ON THE FACE OF THE DEEP

The Sea in Scripture

STUDIES IN BIBLICAL ARCHAEOLOGY, GEOGRAPHY, AND HISTORY

Barry J. Beitzel, series editor

Ahab's House of Horrors: A Historiographic Study of the Military Campaigns of the House of Omri
by Kyle R. Greenwood and David B. Schreiner

On the Face of the Deep: The Sea in Scripture
by Linford Stutzman

Where Was the Biblical Red Sea? Examining the Ancient Evidence
by Barry J. Beitzel

"Reading this beautifully written book helped me appreciate even more all the stories behind many of the fascinating places we visited while sailing our own sailboat around the Eastern Mediterranean over the past three years. *Loved it!*"

—**Kay Finley**, owner and skipper of sailing yacht *Mai Tai*

"A valuable contribution to an understanding of travel on the seas during the biblical eras. Stutzman has rightly highlighted the importance of maritime trade and travel in ancient cultures. He provides excellent descriptions of sailors, sailing vessels, ports, and the economic importance of trade on the waterways. The dangers and difficulties of travel and trade on the seas are set in the context of the potential financial benefits or losses incurred by the merchants and owners of the vessels. The book is interspersed with interesting personal anecdotes from the author's twenty years of sailing along the coasts of Greece, Turkey, and Israel."

—**Mark R. Fairchild**, Huntington University, Indiana (retired);
author of *The Underwater Basilica of Nicaea: Archaeology in the Birthplace of Christian Theology*

"With one hand on the Bible and the other on the helm of a boat, Stutzman takes the reader on intriguing tours of the Sea of Galilee and the Mediterranean through the lens of Scripture. A New Testament scholar and a seasoned sailor, the author gives rare and rich perspectives on reading the New Testament with Jesus and his disciples on small fishing vessels and with Paul on his international journeys. An enjoyable read that will give the student of the Bible new and fresh vistas into familiar stories."

—**James K. Hoffmeier**, Trinity Evangelical Divinity School, Illinois (emeritus)

"What an incredibly written and researched insight into the sea and its people in Scripture! I am amazed at the way this book opens wide some of the stories we know so well through this unique lens. It has helped add so much color and richness to some of the black-and-white texts. As a passionate sailor and lover of the Word, I so look forward to digesting this in small chunks over and over again. Through Linford's lived experience and meticulous academic study, this is a unique work for all those who love the sea!"

—**Dale Smyth**, race director, Clipper Ventures PLC

"Although it is often unstated, the sea looms large in the minds and cultural worlds of the biblical authors. In this gem of a book, readers are trained to see the waterborne contexts and peoples of the Bible in new and illuminating ways. With Stutzman—a seasoned sailor-scholar—as guide, readers learn to engage Scripture and the life of faith from the perspective of the sea and those who traveled it. The promise of transformative ways of seeing and being in the world await those who undertake the voyage."

—**Eric M. Trinka**, Emory & Henry University, Virginia; author of *Cultures of Mobility, Migration, and Religion in Ancient Israel and Its World*

"A compelling nautical journey through the Scriptures that is rich with historical background, biblical insights, and personal reflections. Drawing on long years of firsthand experience plying the Mediterranean in the aptly named vessel *SailingActs*, Stutzman here traces the biblical story of the people of God from Genesis to Revelation as they move from their land-based origins to engage, in an increasingly vital fashion, with 'the sea and its people.' We owe Stutzman a debt of gratitude for his patient and passionate work at researching and demonstrating the significance of the sea as a crucial historical, theological, and missiological motif throughout the Scriptures."

—**Dorothy Jean Weaver**, Eastern Mennonite Seminary, Virginia (emerita)

"Stutzman challenges Bible readers to make a paradigm shift: to read the text from the perspective of the sea rather than the land. With a broad sweep he surveys Jewish and Greco-Roman history to show how the sea played a prominent role in these ancient societies, their traditions, and their texts. Stutzman sprinkles the text with personal anecdotes related to his two decades of sailing the Mediterranean with his wife, Janet, sharing insider knowledge especially related to the sea journeys of Paul. All aboard for a great read!"

—**Mark Wilson**, director of Asia Minor Research Center, Turkey; Stellenbosch University; University of South Africa

"Stutzman invites us to take a seaward view of Scripture—a gaze long overdue in biblical studies. In the end, the sea is transformed from a metaphor for chaos, impurity, and danger into a metaphor for the unstable and perilous yet promising life through which we all sail. Stutzman's observations spring from texts, geography, archaeology, and his own years of experience sailing the sea routes of the apostle Paul on the Great Sea, the Mediterranean. This is a delightful read—personal, engaging, and as fresh as the deep-sea breezes that beckon us outward."

—**Paul H. Wright**, Jerusalem University College, Israel (emeritus)

ON THE FACE OF THE DEEP

The Sea in Scripture

LINFORD STUTZMAN

Baker Academic
a division of Baker Publishing Group
Grand Rapids, Michigan

Published by Baker Academic
a division of Baker Publishing Group
Grand Rapids, Michigan
BakerAcademic.com

Printed in the United States of America

Library of Congress Cataloging-in-Publication Data
Names: Stutzman, Linford, 1950– author
Title: On the face of the deep : the sea in Scripture / Linford Stutzman.
Description: Grand Rapids, Michigan : Baker Academic, a division of Baker Publishing Group, [2026] | Series: Studies in biblical archaeology, geography, and history | Includes appendix. | Includes bibliographical references and indexes.
Identifiers: LCCN 2025053311 | ISBN 9781540971395 paper | ISBN 9781493457052 ebook | ISBN 9781493457069 pdf
Subjects: LCSH: Sea in the Bible | Bible stories | Sea stories—Mediterranean Region
Classification: LCC BS680.S35 S78 2026
LC record available at https://lccn.loc.gov/2025053311

Baker Publishing Group publications use paper produced from sustainable forestry practices and postconsumer waste whenever possible.

26 27 28 29 30 31 32 7 6 5 4 3 2 1

To all those who go down to the sea in ships.
To Immanuel, Liana, Nathanael.
May you fearlessly navigate both the beauty and the storms of life.

CONTENTS

ILLUSTRATIONS

FIGURES

MAPS

TABLES

PREFACE

I began my life as a landlubber. I saw the ocean for the first time when I was five years old. Our family lived in the Cascade foothills, about a two-hour drive from the small coastal settlement of Newport, Oregon, on the rugged edge of the Pacific Ocean. My father, whose income from logging and farming just kept the family of seven clothed and fed and who also pastored a small church in our community of Cascadia, seldom had time for a vacation. But somehow on that unforgettable day, Dad had not only squeezed in a day at the coast but squeezed the entire family into our 1950 Ford sedan.

I stared in awe and astonishment out across the vast Pacific Ocean with giant breakers smashing the rocks. I could not even see the other side! "Where does it end?" I asked.

"It doesn't really," Dad replied, "but if you went far enough on this ocean you would reach Japan or anywhere else in the world."

I tried to imagine Japan across the endless water and, failing that, settled for wading in the waves along the beach. But from that moment on I dreamed of crossing that ocean one day, all the way to Japan.

The waves on the Oregon coast can be glorious and terrifying as they smash, roaring and foaming, into the rugged rocks that make the place so picturesque. "Where do they come from?" I asked.

"From storms far out at sea," Dad answered.

For years after that encounter with the sea, whenever gale winds caused the tall fir trees to sway and dance outside of our house, I imagined them to be the tall masts of sailing ships in storms at sea.

I have never sailed to Japan or experienced a storm on a boat in the Pacific, but the Mediterranean, as the number of ancient shipwrecks attest, has lured and destroyed the lives of many daring, foolhardy, desperate soldiers, sailors, traders, and slaves. It lured me too.

For most of the years of my life since viewing the ocean in Oregon, I have lived far from the Pacific Ocean: Germany, Australia, Israel, Greece, and Turkey. I have been awed by the beauty of human achievements throughout history, the power of ancient and contemporary culture, and the deadly storms that destroy civilizations.

But mostly I have become fascinated by the sea, particularly the Mediterranean Sea, and by the drama of its people in history and Scripture.

INTRODUCTION

While Genesis 1 to Acts 12 is a story written to, by, and about people who lived in hills, mountains, and deserts of the "biblical lands," almost all of the New Testament from Acts 13 to the end of Revelation was written to, by, and about people who lived in Mediterranean seaports. Paul spent the majority of his life, before and after the Damascus Road encounter with Jesus, in seaports or cities within close proximity to the Mediterranean.[1] The early church west of the Land of Israel[2] thrived primarily in port cities of the Mediterranean during the first century.[3] The study of the physical and social context

---

1. Because there are many uncertainties about Paul's life beginning in Tarsus, the time spent in Jerusalem before his conversion, and travels and activities following his conversion and before Barnabas brings him to Antioch, this assertion is my estimation. It is based not only on the record in Acts and references in Paul's Epistles but also on realistic times for all of his recorded sea journeys. We will examine Paul's lifetime on land and sea more closely in chapter 4.

2. There are many ways to refer to the "Land of Promise" in Scripture and history, depending on who is doing the referring. When practical I will use some form of Land unless another name is commonly used during a specific era. In general, I will use "the Land," "Promised Land," or "Land of Israel" when speaking from a Hebrew point of view until other terms are more helpful.

3. See Rodney Stark, *Cities of God: The Real Story of How Christianity Became an Urban Movement* (San Francisco: HarperSanFrancisco, 2006). Stark correlates several variables and calculates that, of cities having a Christian community by AD 100, sixty-four percent were port cities, compared to twenty-four inland cities. See Stark, *Cities of God*, 225–40. In this study, I include "port cities" as those cities with primary connections to the sea. These are often not directly on the sea but within a day's journey by river or good roads to the seaport. Examples of such seaport cities mentioned in the New Testament are Corinth, Philippi, Antioch on the Orontes, and Paul's hometown of Tarsus. Port cities close to both an excellent harbor and primary roads were some of the most powerful, wealthy cities of the Roman Empire. In the first

of Scripture, however, is primarily land-focused. Yet the sea and its people are always there, sometimes included in the stories. The sea and its people shape the story in both the Hebrew and the Greek Scriptures, but in radically different ways which we will examine in this volume.[4] The collective oral memory of creation, later incorporated into the Hebrew Scriptures, begins, as do other ancient creation accounts, with sea and chaos (Gen 1:1). God's creative acts bring order to this chaos and life begins. The division of the waters (מַיִם, *māyim*) above from the waters below comprises several acts early in the creation sequence (Gen 1:6–9). This division of the waters and dry land is the condition for human life to exist.

The description of the waters that existed before creation can be experienced to this day, the only part described in the creation story that remains essentially the same before and after the third day. While limited by boundaries now, they are first called "sea" in Genesis 1:26 (יָם, *yām*) when on the sixth day of creation Adam is created and given dominion over the fish of the sea. He is not given dominion over the sea itself. Adam and his descendants will indeed be fruitful and multiply, even subdue the earth, but never the sea. And while the Hebrew Scriptures describe an abundance of subduing enemies and obstacles on land, God alone has dominion over the sea. Noah and the flood and Moses and the children of Israel at the Red Sea demonstrate the ambivalence and sometimes negative assumptions about the sea that run through the Hebrew Scriptures. The negative attitudes toward

century, inhabitants of these cities, whether slave or free, male or female, Jew or Greek, were the most well-connected people in the empire, and probably in the entire world.

4. I will not be making the case for "geographic determinism" in this study, but I will examine the differences between the ways that the people of the land viewed the sea and its people in Scripture. The Hebrew and Greek Scriptures were written in the context of interactions of geographically contrasting cultures—Promised Landlubbers and perilous Seafarers. For a popular classic and controversial study of the essential importance of geography in shaping culture and history, Jared Diamond's *Guns, Germs, and Steel: The Fates of Human Societies* (New York: Norton, 2005) is a fascinating read. As a believer in the God revealed in Scripture and the human freedom of choice, I believe culture, history, religion, and Scripture are more fascinating, complex, and unpredictable than Diamond maintains.

the sea extend increasingly to the people who have adapted to it and who threaten Israel's identity and security.

Scripture is shaped by this perspective, and biblical scholars seem to share the bias of the biblical writers about the sea and its people. From the perspective of the land-based authors of the Hebrew Scriptures, the people at home on the sea were almost always enemies. This extends into the New Testament period, as the enticing threat of seaborne Hellenism, followed by the occupation of Rome, reinforced the view of the Mediterranean as a pagan sea. The physical and spiritual lives of the inhabitants of Judea were both threatened by the people who were at home on and around the Mediterranean Sea.[5]

There are many other reasons the Mediterranean Sea, and especially the people who worked on its ships and in its seaports, is rarely the focus of biblical study. While the archaeological sites of the people who inhabited the Promised Land and the neighboring regions contain material remains for archaeologists and biblical scholars to examine, marine archaeology is far more difficult. Wooden ships disintegrate rapidly in the marine environment. The material remains that do exist are generally accessible only to skilled divers with expensive equipment. And while marine archaeologists continue to explore what is accessible, their findings are often not obviously relevant to biblical scholars. This land bias in archaeology is, justifiably, reflected in biblical scholarship.

Further, textual insights into the social world of the sea workers are difficult. Sea workers tended to be illiterate, mobile, and poor.[6] These nonelites of the Roman Empire were, and continue to be, "invisible."

---

5. The generic "waters" of the creation account become the "sea" or "seas" in Scripture. The use of "sea" without any other designation refers increasingly to what will eventually be called the Mediterranean Sea. This is the sea that impacts the life and imagination of the writers of the Hebrew Scriptures after the exodus.

6. Articles discovered in shipwrecks give some limited insight into the sailor's life aboard, coping with boredom, loneliness, and fear. Board games and playing pieces, musical instruments, and amulets were found in the Antikythera shipwreck. Anastasia Gadolou, "Life on Board," in *The Antikythera Shipwreck: The Ship, the Treasures, the Mechanism*, ed. Nikolaos Kaltsas, Elena Vlachogianni, and Polyxeni Bouyia (Athens: Hellenic Ministry of Culture and Tourism, National Archaeological Museum, 2012), 50–57.

As Robert Knapp writes in his book *Invisible Romans,* "The elite of the Roman Empire—emperors, senators, equestrians, and the local elite of magistrates, town councilors, and priests—produced almost all the literature and extraordinary material culture which is commonly spoken of as 'Roman.'"[7] Knapp examines the lives of ordinary men and women, with special attention to the categories of the poor, slaves, freedmen, soldiers, prostitutes, gladiators, bandits, and pirates. It is to this silent majority we turn later.

The Gospels and Acts are rare exceptions to the official written history of the empire. They provide extremely important perspectives from the nonelite inhabitants of the Roman Empire, especially people who used boats or who never made the news unless they caused trouble for Rome. In the Gospels and Acts, these are the key players! The story of the Christian movement in the Mediterranean in Acts is a unique document in which the elites and the nonelites both have voices. The story of Paul is a rare example of an elite Roman citizen who bridged the cultural divide personally by identifying with and relating to both elites and nonelites at the same time.

Later in this volume, I will argue that it is the "invisible" sea workers who are struggling to survive and flourish in a brutal world divided by class, social status, and gender, and controlled and manipulated by promises and threats of the ruling elites, to whom Paul deliberately relates, with whom he identifies, and to whom he addresses his letters. Paul relates to sea workers closely during his longest periods of ministry in the "sordid and dangerous" port cities such as Corinth and Ephesus. It is especially the sea workers who, I will argue, play a significant part in Paul's developing theology of the kingdom, especially his ecclesiology in these port cities. This is because Paul, against all norms of the first century, is, among other things, a seasoned Mediterranean sailor. Paul is a sea-oriented, well-educated, observant Jewish follower of Jesus. There is hardly anyone else with that combination of credentials in the first-century Mediterranean world!

---

7. Robert Knapp, *Invisible Romans* (Cambridge, MA: Harvard University Press, 2011), 10.

Since 2004 my wife and I have been sailing the New Testament world in the Mediterranean. At the time of this writing in 2024, we have now lived for twenty years aboard *SailingActs,* our old sailboat we call home for six months each year. We have read and reread the biblical sea stories on the unpredictable waters of the Mediterranean, surrounded by the descendants of Greeks, Romans, Philistines, Jews, Phoenicians, pirates, slaves, and seafarers who live around its rim, as well as the modern, polyglot nomads of the sea from countries like South Africa, Russia, Australia, Sweden, Germany, Spain, and a host of others. This prolonged "immersion" in the sea world of Scripture has changed not only our perspectives but our lives as well. I suspect this is what happened to everyone in the biblical sea stories, including those of the seafarers who are actors in the biblical stories but whose voices are seldom recorded in them.

In the chapters that follow, I will use the key references to the sea in Scripture in roughly the order in which they occur from Genesis to Revelation. These are mostly familiar stories and perspectives for biblical readers and scholars. What is less familiar is what lies beneath the surface of the sea stories: weather patterns, trade routes, politics, and especially the characteristics and social lives of the seafarers.

Both the Hebrew and the Greek Scriptures are shaped by the sea but in vastly different ways. Several conclusions about the sea in Scripture emerge out of these years of experiences on *SailingActs.* We sailed the Roman sea routes that Paul did. We visited all of the seaports mentioned in Acts. This experience, combined with the research of archaeologists (including those working in the relatively new field of marine archaeology), historians, sociologists, biblical scholars, and experts in other areas of Mediterranean studies, leads me to conclude the following: The sea stories in Scripture are extremely important, for they connect with universal themes that shape the culture of the modern world, of which we are part.

But because these familiar sea stories are told from the perspective of the Promised Landlubbers with their land-shaped and grounded faith, we take their perspective. Those who go "down to the sea in ships" (Ps 107:23) may include Jews, but they are likely not very typical ones, for seafarers are usually depicted as the losers or the villains in the biblical stories. But these sea workers who sailed the merchant and navy ships, labored in the seaports, and moved constantly at great personal risk helped shape the Western, global culture of which we are a part. They were part of the early Christian communities in the bustling port cities. They carried stories and ideas with them, including the gospel, in their constant movement throughout the Mediterranean.

In contrast to the heroes of the Hebrew Scriptures, both Jesus and Paul were seagoing "heroes" who related closely to seagoing "losers," of which we are part culturally and theologically.

Therefore, we need to reread the sea stories in Scripture, listening with imagination informed by history, marine archaeology, ancient texts, and the cultural and physical environment of the Mediterranean itself, listening for the voices of the mostly illiterate sea workers in those stories. Informed imagination can help us better understand and appreciate the people who were at home on the sea, especially on the Mediterranean Sea.

Understanding and appreciating the seafarers of the Mediterranean in the biblical story can help us understand and appreciate the bold, boundary-shattering message and actions of Jesus and the fearless, land- and sea-wandering genius of Paul, who connected the message of Jesus to the disparate groups of people living around the Mediterranean Sea.

Insight into the social dynamics of the seaports in those famously wealthy and raucous cities like Ephesus and Corinth, shaped by fierce division and conflict between the sea workers and the wealthy elite, will help us recognize the relevance of the Acts story and Paul's Epistles to the inhabitants of those seaports. More importantly, rereading the biblical sea stories with informed imagination can help those of us who live in our Mediterranean-shaped, unstable, unpredictable, functionally pagan global culture and future to live faithfully and to connect the good news of the kingdom of God to all people in our hyperconnected world.

The sea and Scripture are both deep. The exploration of both sea and Scripture is a lifetime, inexhaustible opportunity of deeply satisfying, even risky exploration, for encounters with either or both can change one's life. Both the sea and Scripture are, as Rudolf Otto famously states in describing the numinous, or divine power, *mysterium tremendum et fascinans*—an awe-inspiring mystery that is at once terrifying and attractive in its magnificent beauty, inscrutable depths, and powerful promise.[8] The lure of both pulls us toward awe and wonder, respect and fear, that can give freedom and profound fearlessness of anything else.

This volume is limited to outlining the perception of the sea and its people in Scripture and the significance of that view to people of faith. As such, it is a short voyage on the face of the deep.

REFLECTIONS FROM THE SEA

To sail the Mediterranean following the sea routes of the apostle Paul had been a dream of mine for years and finally was made possible thanks to a fifteen-month sabbatical from Eastern Mennonite University (EMU). I had become convinced after leading EMU's undergraduate cross-cultural study program in the Middle East for several previous semesters that to better understand and appreciate the biblical story in its context I would "need to read the Bible with your feet," as Paul Wright, then president of the Jerusalem University College, would often tell our students. My experiences of hiking the Jesus Trail under the blazing sun, taking shelter from downpours in a Dead Sea Scroll cave at Qumran, and needing to alter travel plans to Gaza due to yet

8. Rudolf Otto introduced this central idea in his book *Das Heilige* in 1917. Rudolf Otto, *The Idea of the Holy*, trans. John W. Harvey (Oxford: Oxford University Press, 1923).

another security alert added to my understanding and appreciation of Abraham, Samuel, Jesus, and Paul in their social and geographical environment. To walk the Bible on the Land with the heroes of faith helped make my imagination realistic. The experiential connection to the Land and its people helped me understand and appreciate how the Hebrew writers viewed the sea and its people.

It was during a short boat excursion from Kibbutz Ein Gev on the Sea of Galilee with the Jerusalem University seminar when it occurred to me that I had left the Land of the Hebrew Scriptures and had launched into the Greek world of the New Testament Scriptures by stepping aboard that boat. Once aboard, I realized that I would need to read the Bible from a boat on the Sea of Galilee to better appreciate Jesus and his fishermen disciples and the significance of Jesus' choice of a fishing village as the base of his ministry. I might even have to sail with Paul on the Mediterranean Sea to understand the world of the Greek New Testament in which Paul was at home.

Shortly thereafter on the same seminar, while gazing west toward Rome from the ancient harbor of Caesarea, the seed was planted. I would write my proposal for my upcoming sabbatical to sail the routes of Paul recorded in Acts, explore all thirty-seven named seaports and nine islands visited by Paul on those journeys, and share what I learned through my research, preparation, and experience of traveling with Paul on land and sea. When, with some trepidation, I related the "vision" to my wife, Janet, I was overjoyed that she immediately got on board!

In writing the sabbatical proposal, I encountered the bias described above by the committee reviewing it. How does sailing the Mediterranean Sea contribute to biblical studies?

"Good question," I told the committee. "A similar kind of question some of the early believers from Jerusalem most likely asked Paul and Barnabas before they launched west from Antioch."

The committee approved the proposal! Immediately life changed dramatically for Janet and me. While the change from land to sea was not nearly as profound as the impact on world history that began when Paul and his companions left by ship from Antioch's port, Seleucia, it has been for us like it seems to have been for Paul and those who sailed with him—a voyage of learning. We did not take that sabbatical. The sabbatical took us.

FIGURE 1: **Winter 2005 in Ashkelon, Israel**

CHAPTER 1

DIVISION: WATER, SEA, LAND, AND PEOPLE IN THE HEBREW SCRIPTURES

"And God said, 'Let the waters under the sky be gathered together into one place, and let the dry land appear.' And it was so. God called the dry land Earth, and the waters that were gathered together he called Seas. And God saw that it was good."
Genesis 1:9–10

THE ANCIENT WATER STORIES

The foundational story in Hebrew Scripture begins with "wind" or "Spirit" (רוּחַ, *rûaḥ*) moving on the face of the "waters" (*māyim*). The late Raphael Patai, in his seminal work on Jewish seafaring, recognized and appreciated the often-overlooked impact of the sea on Jewish literature, including Hebrew Scripture, the Talmud, and Midrash. He traces the evidence of Jewish participation in seafaring beginning with Noah and how this participation impacted Jewish culture and writing. He begins his study: "The Bible, that unique literary masterpiece, opens with an account of the mythical beginnings of the history of the world, of mankind, and of the people of Israel, proceeds with an admixture of myth and history in which the former gradually diminishes as the latter gains ground, and then continues with a theocentric historical account of developments ... [of the people of Israel]."[1]

The biblical account of the creation story can be approached from many different directions. Social historians compare it to other ancient creation myths; theistic evolutionary scientists suggest possible nonliteral interpretations; theologians focus on the foundational assumptions of creation that are developed throughout the entire Scriptures. The perspective of this volume is focused on water, the divisions between water and land, the divergent views of the people of the land and the people of the sea toward water, and finally how these geographic divisions between people of sea and land shape history and the faith story of God's people. The divisions in the creation story on which the Hebrew Scriptures rest provide the foundational worldview about the Creator, the universe, all of life, and humans, who bear the image of the Creator.

CREATION

In the beginning was water and chaos. On this, the Hebrew creation stories agree with Egyptian, Babylonian, and many other creation stories around the world. The first creative acts of God bring order to this chaos and life begins. The division between land and water is the first of the several acts of division early in the Hebrew account of creation. These divisions provide the conditions for human life.

---

1. Raphael Patai, *The Children of Noah: Jewish Seafaring in Ancient Times* (Princeton, NJ: Princeton University Press, 1998), 3. While I do not refer to the biblical creation story as "myth," I understand Patai's use of the term here as the collective and selective memory of a people's origins that explain the source and meaning of life, human identity, and their responsibilities. Patai's differentiation between "myth" and "history" does not mean that one is true and the other is not. It simply distinguishes between stories that can be considered "prehistory," originating outside of the time frame of human record. The creation story is truth that is embraced by faith.

FIGURE 2: **Sunrise on the southern Turkish coast**

The Hebrew writers of Scripture are all people of the land.[2] Until Paul wrote his early letters, and Luke wrote his Gospel and Acts, the sea was generally seen as a foreign, sometimes forbidding, and dangerous world. Yes, God created both the waters and the land and pronounced them good in the creation story. The Creator was the ruler over all creation, including the waters of the sea. These are primary theological affirmations of creation. Historically, however, while the Mediterranean was a sea of promise for the people of the sea, it was often a sea of peril for the Jewish people of the Land in their experience with the sea and its people.[3] Fluid, changeable, capricious, and

2. In this study I will use "land" generically for the Hebrew people as being land-oriented in both their experience and theology. When referring to the geographical context of the Hebrew Scriptures in the "Land of Promise," I will use "Land." The Hebrew word אֶרֶץ (*ʾereṣ*) is used far more often than the sea in the Hebrew Scriptures but has a broader scope of applications ranging from the entire earth, the part of the earth not covered by waters, specific territories, and, commonly, the Land of Israel. *ʾEreṣ* is used 2,504 times. In the Greek New Testament, γῆ (*gē*) is the most common word for land, used 252 times.

3. The designation of the "sea" in Scripture almost always refers to the Mediterranean Sea unless other seas are identified explicitly. The name "Mediterranean" comes much later than the Hebrew Scriptures. The names of the Mediterranean in antiquity given by the people who lived around it will be discussed later. I will use "Mediterranean" for specificity and clarity, when necessary, before the introduction of the name in history.

chaotic, the Mediterranean and the people who sailed it were viewed as an unpredictable counterpart to the steadfast, unmovable character of God, the Land, and the people who had been promised it.

There is a consistency in the use of the terms "waters" (*māyim*) and "sea" (*yām*) used in the creation story and the entire Hebrew Scripture. "Sea" almost always refers to a bounded body of water that can be identified by name.[4] "Waters," on the other hand, usually connotes unbounded, unfathomable depth and chaos. And when the two terms are used together, as in the "waters of the sea" in which the Egyptians perished while pursuing the Israelites (Exod 15:19) or in the description of judgments pronounced by Amos (Amos 9:6), "waters" are the untamed, life-threatening, destructive part of creation that remains under the dominion of God alone, even when they are waters of a specific sea. In the flood account (Gen 7–8), it is the "waters" that destroy life. "Sea" is not used in the flood story at all. Finally, there are several positive usages of the "waters/sea" combination. In Psalm 33 the writer extols the greatness of God as the one who controls the waters and the sea. About the power displayed in the creation, he writes, "He gathered the waters of the sea as in a bottle; he put the deeps in storehouses" (Ps 33:7).

The prophet Isaiah foresees a time of peace and justice instituted by God following his judgment against the wicked (Isa 11). Both Isaiah and Habakkuk describe the universal rule of God as a time when "the earth will be filled with the knowledge of the glory of the LORD, as the waters cover the sea" (Hab 2:14; compare Isa 11:9).

Thus, the divisions of water and land described in the story of creation provide a basic understanding of God as the divider of the waters from the land. And while God is the absolute and only ruler of both, and both are pronounced "good," the implicit sense is that the land is the part of creation for humans. The sea is for other species.

---

4. There are many names of seas in Scripture: the Red Sea (יַם־סוּף, *yam-sûp*) and various names of the Dead Sea, such as the "salt sea" (Gen 14:3; יָם הַמֶּלַח, *yām hammelaḥ*), the "east sea" (Joel 2:20; יָם הַקַּדְמֹנִי, *yām haqqadmōnî*), and the "sea of the plain" (Josh 3:16; יָם הָעֲרָבָה, *yām hāʿărābâ*).

This understanding of God undergirded the self-identity of the people of the land and the way they perceived the people of the sea and their gods. The God of the Land and the gods of the sea were viewed from the perspective of the geographical environment of the people of the land and the people of the sea. The division between land and sea is a geographical reality forming a widening cultural division between people of the sea and people of the land.

The contrasts between the land people and sea people are developed through the Hebrew Scriptures based on the writers' limited firsthand experience with the sea, their eventual encounter with seafarers, and perhaps some vivid imagination and fear of the unknown. While the enemies of the Hebrews in the Land are both land-based and sea-based, the presence of sea-based enemies is the most threatening for the longest time. The contrasting perceptions of the sea are related to the differing perspectives of the peoples of the sea and of the land toward everything else—the world, God, themselves, and each other.

The geographically shaped view of the gods of the seafaring people, as described in both history and the Hebrew Scriptures, mirrors the view of the sea. Both the sea and the gods of the sea can be characterized as capricious, temperamental, beautiful, violent, sullen, and volatile. The images and reputation of the gods even travel the sea on trading and military vessels, competing with and eventually joining the existing local gods in a growing pantheon of Mediterranean deities. These seagoing gods share common identities under a variety of local names. The sea carries the promises of the various pagan gods, offering personal power and success in all its forms—knowledge, beauty, victory, safety, health, wealth, pleasure, long life, honor, and status. For the people of the land, the seductive gods of the sea, like the sea itself, are perilous.

In contrast, the God of the Old Testament is faithful and changeless. God is a rock. He reveals himself to his people among the sand and craggy rocks of the Sinai. He gives his commandments to Moses on the top of a mountain. This is a God who is seldom described with sea metaphors nor is identified with the sea. God does not make his dwelling place in the seas as Poseidon, nor emerge from the sea as Aphrodite. Just as God divides the water from the land in the third act of creation and calls it good, the division of the people of the sea and the people of the land is also good, for God dwells primarily on land. To be close to God, his people dwell there too.

Creation is the foundational story upon which the entire Hebrew Scriptures are built. The story of the Great Flood reinforces the creation accounts of divisions: water and land; sea and land; the wicked and the righteous; life and death.

THE GREAT FLOOD

Patai's history of Jewish seafaring identifies the story of the Great Flood (Gen 6–9) as not only the first seafaring story in Hebrew Scripture but a story with foundational theological implications. He writes, "The Bible, in consistency with the mythical traditions of many ancient peoples, presents the story of a primeval great flood that wiped out mankind except for a few persons, who survived in some sort of watercraft."[5] Stories of a great flood, with the gods instructing the building of a vessel to survive it, are found in several creation accounts of ancient peoples.[6] Patai notes, "The ancient Hebrews constituted no exception in attributing the construction of the first watercraft to a builder who followed divine instruction. According to the Book of Genesis, it was God himself who gave instructions to Noah, the first and only shipbuilder mentioned in the Bible."[7]

The traditional location of the Garden of Eden between the Tigris and Euphrates Rivers, the cryptic account of the descendants of Cain wandering eastward, and the location of Mount Ararat give the traditional general location of the inhabitants saved and destroyed in the flood. This study will focus, as with the creation story, on the water

5. Patai, *Children of Noah*, 3.

6. The Sumerian deluge myth and the Akkadian epic of Gilgamesh are two examples cited by Patai.

7. Patai, *Children of Noah*, 4.

and land features of the story that reinforce creation-based assumptions about God, land and sea, good and evil, and human identity and responsibility.

With the freedom of humans created in God's image to consider and then act on the attractive idea that they could indeed become "like God, knowing good and evil" (Gen 3:5), the human horror of the deep, chaotic waters of Genesis is experienced again. As the chaos of the "deep" is the pre-creation condition, the resetting of creation begins again with mighty waters. If the separation of water from dry land and the establishment of boundaries to keep them in their place in the creation story is "good," this story of the flood is the opposite. According to the biblical account, preparing for an unknown phenomenon such as a flood by building an unnecessary boat on dry land over many years of meteorological stability would have seemed an absurdity, and Noah and his family, misfits. Imagine the endless chattering, arguments, and jokes of everyone who observed or heard about Noah's building project and the reasons for it. For land-based societies, the future is as stable as the past. The waters have their place. The bounded waters, it seems, are as predictable as the land, as life itself. So everyone besides Noah's family is depicted as being confidently corrupt. They are surely talking incessantly, congratulating themselves for being in control, living without restraint, dominating, exploiting, laughing at Noah and his pathetic righteousness, his stubborn stupidity. The relational division among the descendants of Adam and Eve is, like the division of the waters and the land, deep. The waters in the flood story are no longer divided by the Creator. The waters, under the control of the Creator as always, divide humanity—the righteous family who follows God's instructions and survives by building a boat, and the rest of the human family who drowns in the waters. The family on the boat gets the attention, with Noah getting most of it. So while the fall in the creation story unites the human family in its consequences, the story of the flood divides it.

Then the waters recede, the sun dries out the land, and the rainbow appears. God promises not to curse the earth with water again no matter how evil humanity becomes: "As long as the earth endures, seedtime and harvest, cold and heat, summer and winter, day and night, shall not cease" (Gen 8:22). While it is likely that Noah and his family accepted this promise with great relief, there is no record of his verbal response. The only quote from Noah in the entire story is at the very end. His seafaring behind him, Noah is again "a man of the soil" (Gen 9:20). After he has planted a vineyard, makes wine, and unexpectedly becomes very intoxicated, Noah awakes in shame and anger and says, "Cursed be Canaan" (Gen 9:25). That's it. No other commentary from Noah in the entire flood story beyond the curse of Canaan (Ham), which Noah then follows with blessings for Canaan's other brothers, Shem and Japheth (Gen 9:26–27).

The descendants of the three sons of Noah will remember and relate to the waters of the sea differently in history. Noah's three sons, Shem, Ham, and Japheth, are mentioned as the three primary families migrating in different directions. A descendant of Javan (Japheth) is identified as the ancestor of the people of the coastlands such as Tarshish and Kittim (Cyprus) (Gen 10:4).

Thus, the flood narrative is another foundational story on which the Hebrew understanding of the good division of land and the waters is the template for good/evil human divisions. What changes as the waters recede, the rainbow appears, the land dries out, and the descendants of Noah's family again are fruitful and multiply?

Following the story of Babel, humanity divides linguistically, then, inevitably, geographically. From the evidence of the earliest human migration patterns, cultural differences become established and evolve regionally as the migrants adapt to their natural environment. The migrating humans who make their home in proximity to the sea eventually understand the world, themselves, and others differently from those who make their home inland.

The remaining water and sea stories from Hebrew Scripture in this chapter are mostly negative about both the sea and its people. They are also much easier to ground in human history and geographical location. The perspective of the foundational stories toward the sea and its people is maintained and expanded through key sea narratives of the Hebrew Scriptures.

STORIES OF WATER, SEA, AND SEAFARERS

The next five stories take a cursory look at the historical, geographical, and cultural context of the Hebrews and the non-Hebrew actors in the stories in the order they appear in Scripture. The primary focus will be on how the Hebrews understand the sea and its people, how they relate to them, and how their interpretations and memories of their experiences with the sea and its people are woven into Hebrew Scripture. These key sea-related stories rest on the stories of creation and the flood. All reinforce the narrative of the Hebrews' land-based identity in contrast to the seafarers. The stories are the exodus from Egypt, the conflict with the Philistines, the sea dominance and interactions with the Phoenicians, the judgment of Tyre, and the story of Jonah. All of these stories are the subjects of intense scrutiny and debate. The descriptions of the exodus of the Hebrew people and their encounters with the Philistines are primarily based on the Hebrew Scriptures, while the Phoenicians are much better known from extrabiblical texts and material evidence.[8] These stories, likely sharing the same approximate historical era, all depict the interaction of the Hebrew people with the sea, its people, or both.

EGYPT, THE NILE, THE EXODUS, AND THE RED SEA

The exodus saga (Exod 14–15), with the miraculous escape through the waters of the Red Sea (*yam-sûp*), begins along the water. It is a confrontation between the Hebrew landlubbers and the Egyptian Empire, built along the great Nile River and at home on it.[9]

8. The excavations in Ashkelon and Gath in Israel from 1985 to 2016 have produced fresh insight into Philistine culture. See the section on the Philistines below.

9. While Old Kingdom Egypt was highly developed and might be assumed to be the first naval power in the Mediterranean, "the Egyptians regarded the shores of the Mediterranean as the outer edge of their world, which was defined by the Nile, not by the sea beyond." David Abulafia, *The Great Sea: A Human History of the Mediterranean* (Oxford: Oxford University Press, 2011), 22. The Hebrew Scriptures do not use the name "Nile." "The river of Egypt" (נְהַר מִצְרַיִם,

According to Herodotus, "Egypt is the gift of the Nile," for the Nile was the key to the production and distribution of everything necessary to build an amazing empire.[10] The Nile is the river of life in Egypt. The integration of Upper and Lower Egypt and the resources required to build the powerful and durable Egyptian Empire required organization and specialists, including those who developed and sailed the first boats built of the plentiful reeds and later wooden versions with unique rigging adapted for plying the waters up and down the Nile River.[11] These sailboats, with their triangular lateen sails, are still used on the Nile. The feluccas could utilize the winds blowing upriver and the currents of the Nile flowing down to the Mediterranean. Feluccas on the Nile were able to transport the materials needed to build pyramids and empires. The connection of Upper and Lower Egypt by river transportation is key to the development of this incredible Egyptian civilization. The astonishing level of human achievement included unprecedented construction projects that endure to this day.

Massive building projects require massive labor forces. The supply of paid Egyptian construction workers was sometimes not enough for the pharaoh's ambitious building projects. It was unlikely that Egyptians with other options would choose to do heavy, exhausting, dangerous toil.[12] Non-Egyptian slaves were the obvious solution. So resident Hebrew aliens, descendants of the family of Joseph, were now enslaved to build the domination and reputation of the pharaoh further in Egypt and to expand the rule into new territory. The Nile

---

nəhar miṣrayim) is used in Genesis 15:18, and the story of the exodus simply uses the "river" (*nəhar*), with the context inferring the Nile River.

10. Whenever referring to Egypt and the Nile, it seems necessary to include the observation attributed to Herodotus: "Egypt is the gift of the Nile" (*The Histories*). Flowing south to north for over four thousand miles (6,400 km), the Nile is considered the longest river in the world. A little over nine hundred miles (1,400 km) of the Nile is in present-day Egypt.

11. For a thorough discussion of the evolution of ancient sailing boats and rigging, see Lionel Casson, *Ships and Seamanship in the Ancient World* (Baltimore, MD: The Johns Hopkins University Press, 1995), especially pages 11–20 which detail the development of the early Nile River seacraft.

12. The exception may have been construction projects, including the pyramids, that were done by paid volunteers during the flood season of the year when farm work was minimal.

FIGURE 3: **Feluccas on the Nile River in Cairo, Egypt**

flows through the narrative from the arrival of Joseph as a slave to the birth of Moses, the plagues, and the exodus itself.[13] The exodus account opens with the new pharaoh "who did not know Joseph" conscripting the Hebrews for the ambitious building projects of the cities Pithom and Ramses (Exod 1:8–14).[14] Since these cities were built next to the Nile, building materials could be delivered there from their sources comparatively easily. The Nile is the river of life

13. Water is life throughout Scripture. The so-called Fertile Crescent is defined by water—rivers and rainfall. The green parts of the maps of the Fertile Crescent begin in Mesopotamia ("between rivers"), extend south to present-day Lebanon with its reliable precipitation in the mountains, and then fade to brown through Canaan, which lacks both a useful river and reliable rainfall. Egypt, at the southern tip of the Crescent, is a narrow strip of green along the Nile River.

14. Debate around the exodus account as even being a historical event, or around details in the scriptural account such as dating, geographic details, and the lack of non-biblical textual verification, continue. For a good summary of some of the debates and possible evidence, see James K. Hoffmeier, "Out of Egypt," *Biblical Archaeology Review* 33 (2007): 30–37, 39–41.

and posterity for the Egyptian rulers and the river of grinding toil until death for the enslaved Hebrews.

Until, that is, the story of Moses. Here not only is the Nile the river of life for the Egyptians, but the life of Moses is also saved on the Nile, thanks to his daring and creative mother (Exod 2:1–10). Rescued by the pharaoh's daughter, Moses grows up next to the Nile River in the pharaoh's family.[15] But he does not stay there. In fleeing to the desert after the murder of an Egyptian taskmaster, where Moses' loyalty to his people deepens, he becomes at home in the barren land of Midian, where once again he is saved by water (Exod 2:15–19). Water is life in Egypt or the wilderness equally.

When Moses returns to Egypt to confront the pharaoh, his first plague strikes directly at the source of Egypt's power, the waters of the Nile (Exod 7:14–24). The source of life for the Egyptians is also the source of death with the very first plague. Like the Hebrew Moses himself, the Egyptians need to be rescued from the water of the Nile. As from the beginning, God, not Pharaoh, controls water. This first plague begins a series of confrontations culminating with the death of Pharaoh's son, the Passover event, and the escape from Egypt. The Hebrew slaves are now free to begin the journey toward the Land, promised to them by God.

But immediately there are sea obstacles. The direct route along the Mediterranean Sea would take the Hebrews through the "land of the Philistines" where "God thought, 'if the people face war, they may change their minds and return to Egypt'" (Exod 13:17). Were the Philistines in the way at that time? The questions of the dating of the arrival of the Philistines will be addressed a bit more in the next section. However, the point here is that in the story, the

15. The choice of Moses' name (מֹשֶׁה, *mōšeh*) is explained by the pharaoh's daughter, "because I drew him out of the water" (Exod 2:10). While other possible sources of this name are debated, it is clear from the Hebrew writers that Moses is named because he was "drawn out" or rescued from the water. Thus, the Nile saves Moses' life, and he lives because he is rescued from it. The very name of Moses, the great leader of the exodus, symbolizes the ambiguity of the relationship of the Hebrews to the waters that could be both destructive and lifegiving, a view reflecting the creation and flood accounts of Scripture.

Philistine sea invaders are in the Land. They are assumed to be armed and dangerous. Later, the Hebrews arriving from the desert will meet their most formidable, tenacious enemies, who had arrived in the Land by sea. Their assumptions about the Philistines will be confirmed.

The entrapment followed by deliverance through the Red Sea demonstrates for the Hebrews the threat of the waters and God's power over them.[16] It is through the sea on *dry* land that God leads his people. Then, fittingly, the sea destroys the Egyptian army.[17] In the wilderness where water is scarce, God provides. God meets Moses at the top of a mountain, and Moses receives God's commandments carved in stone. It is into and through the desert that God leads his people to the Land where everlasting covenants will be realized. While this God may have power over all of nature, God almost always chooses to demonstrate his power on the land where his people belong. This forty-year wilderness interlude between the deliverance through the waters of the Red Sea and the crossing of the waters of the River Jordan into the Promised Land forges the land-based identity of the Hebrews that is reflected in Scripture.

The exodus becomes the key formational story of the self-identity of the Hebrew people, their understanding and covenantal relationship with God, and their purpose of progressing toward the promise. The general assumptions about waters and sea depicted in the creation and flood accounts have been reinforced in this formative

---

16. The entire exodus narrative is the subject of intense scrutiny and debate regarding whether it happened as described in Scripture, and if it did, exactly when and how it occurred; the geographical location of places like the Red Sea, Mount Sinai, and the wilderness; and where the key events in those locations occurred. For an in-depth examination of the debate over the location of the biblical Red Sea, for example, see Barry J. Beitzel, *Where Was the Biblical Red Sea? Examining the Ancient Evidence,* Studies in Biblical Archaeology, Geography, and History (Bellingham, WA: Lexham Press, 2020).

17. The Red Sea is the only sea mentioned by name in both the Hebrew and Greek Scriptures. Including the Apocrypha, the Red Sea is mentioned 74 times. This is second to the Mediterranean, which is called by various names for a total of around 119 times. However, the Red Sea stories refer to a single event in the exodus narrative. The references to the Mediterranean Sea, on the other hand, are about stories over the entire history of the Israelites in the Land, over more than one thousand years of history.

experience of the exodus and the wilderness sojourn. You can take the children of Israel through the Red Sea into the wilderness, but they will be confronted again by another sea in the Land of Promise. This sea will be far more perilous for a much longer time.

THE PHILISTINES, SEAFARERS IN THE LAND

While the Israelites are wandering the Sinai and at last crossing the Jordan River to begin the conquest of the Land under the leadership of Joshua, the Sea Peoples are invading from the sea and establishing themselves in the Canaanite territory of the Land.[18] The Philistines do not seem to need a promise from any god to occupy any new territory they desire. They are seafarers with the confidence of Greeks. They are like the sea and their sea-like gods.[19]

The dating of the Philistines' arrival, like the dating of the exodus itself, is fraught with difficulties, for the dates of both the exodus and the initial arrival of the Philistines are complicated by the contradictions in the dating in Scripture, as well as evidence of archaeology and other scientific means of dating both.[20] Uncertainties aside,

---

18. For an overview of the evidence for Sea Peoples and Philistines, see Abulafia, *The Great Sea*, 42–59. Based on biblical and ancient Egyptian historical accounts, Abulafia describes the invasion of "Sea Peoples" into areas controlled by Egyptian and Hittite rule when they were politically and militarily weak. Philistines were among the Sea Peoples who successfully dominated other areas of the eastern end of the Mediterranean, but after being repulsed by Ramesses III, they settled in on the southern coast of Palestine, where they developed as an independent political entity that posed a threat to the Canaanites of the area and eventually the Hebrew newcomers. Trude and Moshe Dothan assert, "During the same period the Israelites, who had invaded Palestine from the East, were settling in the hill country." Trude Dothan and Moshe Dothan, *People of the Sea: The Search for the Philistines* (New York: Macmillan, 1992), xi (and see the thorough discussion of the Philistines in that volume).

19. This applies to the Philistines and other sea-connected neighbors, including the Phoenicians and the Canaanites of the Levant. Ba'al is the god of the storm, connected with the sea. *Yam* is the Semitic word for "sea" used in Hebrew Scriptures and is also the name of the Canaanite god of the sea representing chaos. Yam was the god of the sea in the pantheon of the Phoenicians, depicted consistently as tyrannical, angry, violent, and harsh. The etymological connection of the god and the sea and the association of the characteristics of both in the Hebrew worldview and experience is clear.

20. The Leon Levy Expedition conducted at ancient Ashkelon, Israel, from 1985 to 2016 yielded a wealth of information about the Philistines not found in Hebrew Scripture. Based on pottery finds and other evidence, Lawrence Stager, lead archaeologist, concludes that the arrival

what is clear is that if the escape through the Red Sea confirms God's power over the waters, the Philistines demonstrate the power of the Sea People over the Great Sea. As mentioned above, this sea-based domination of at least the shores of the Philistine territory is inferred by the Hebrew writers in Exodus 23:31 with the term "the sea of the Philistines" (יָם פְּלִשְׁתִּים, *yām pəlaštîm*). The details of the expansion around the rim of the eastern Mediterranean and the Levant of these intrepid, self-confident invaders from the coastal mainland and islands of the Aegean are the subject of ongoing debate. Their origins, their time frame, and the extent of their eastward conquests by land and sea are all subjects of extensive inquiry in archaeology, research in ancient biblical and nonbiblical texts, and DNA analysis. Although the historicity of the Hebrew Scriptures has been challenged, there is general acceptance that the establishment of the Philistines in the Land coincides with the Hebrews' protracted effort to acquire their promised allotment and to defend themselves against Philistine intrusions into the territory occupied by the Israelites.[21]

FIGURE 4: **Remains of Philistine Ashkelon**

The perspective of the Mediterranean Sea in Hebrew Scriptures is initially derived from its hostile representatives, the Philistines. They

of the Philistines in Ashkelon was around 1175 BC. See Lawrence E. Stager, "When Canaanites and Philistines Ruled Ashkelon," *Biblical Archaeology Review* 17 (1991): 24–29, 31, 35–37, 40–42.

21. The first reference to the "Land of Israel" (אֶרֶץ יִשְׂרָאֵל, *'ereṣ yiśrā'ēl*) is found in 1 Samuel 13:19, and this term will be used as well as "Land" from this point on. I will also normally use "Israelite" in the following text, indicating the Hebrews' arrival and presence in the Land of Israel. Although various other terms refer to the Land in Scripture, for simplicity, I will generally use "Israel" and "Israelite" because of their identity with the Land of Israel after they had arrived. They are called both "Israelites" and "Hebrews" in Scripture.

are mentioned as enemies in conflict with Israel almost as often as all the indigenous enemies combined whom Israel faced in its conquest.[22] They are the sea-wandering pagan newcomers in the Land, the existential, perennial threat to the desert-wandering Hebrew newcomers. They beach their boats on the eastern shores of the Mediterranean at roughly the same time that the Israelites are invading from the desert. The conflicts and confrontations are between the desert nomads seeking freedom from their slavery in Egypt and safety from their enemies on one side, and the seafarers looking for new places to conquer, settle, and develop for their own expansionist reasons on the other. This will not end in a truce. So the endless battles, intrigues, triumphs, and atrocities on both sides are described at length in the Hebrew Scripture, beginning in Judges. Desert sand against sea salt. Pagan worshipers of a whole range of sea-like gods challenging Hebrew worshipers of a single mountain-like God at home in the desert. The tough shepherds and farmers planting vines and fig trees to sit under with their extended families and telling stories of God's faithfulness competing with the tough, bold sailors with their iron swords and chariots who build cities, plant crops in the best agricultural areas, and keep trying to displace the "hillbillies" from Bethlehem and other villages in the hills.

It is a long and pitched battle. Neither side are wimps. Neither side seems to win for long. The Philistines are self-assured because they know they have the best equipment and serve the proven gods of fertility and victory. And they have survived the dangers of the seas to reach the Land of the Hebrews. The Hebrews are just as confident because they know that the God of their ancestors delivers on his promises to them and against their enemies. And they have survived the dangers of the wilderness to reach the Land of Promise.

---

22. The most referenced indigenous enemies of Canaanite tribes, often listed together, are mentioned 280 times compared to 240 times the Philistines are mentioned by themselves. This is only one way to compare the ongoing level of threat of the Philistines following the initial conquest.

The archaeological records and even the biblical descriptions demonstrate that not only the Hebrews but also the Philistines were innovative, creative, triumphant conquerors and builders of cities and economies. The Philistines, like the Israelites, do not suffer from timidity or apologize to their neighbors.

Two key dramatic stories of confrontation between the Philistines and the Israelites, Samson versus the Philistines and David versus Goliath, demonstrate the contrasts between the landlubbers and the seafarers.[23]

Samson

The seduction of Samson was most likely not only a romantic attraction to a beautiful Philistine woman but also an attraction to the exciting culture she represented to a young, headstrong Hebrew living on the margins of Israelite territory. While this may not seem to be immediately important, the boy Samson would likely have been able to catch glimpses of the Mediterranean Sea as he explored the hill country around his village of Zorah, igniting his curiosity and imagination about the sea and its people. Growing up close to Philistine territory and its radically different culture appears to have undermined his loyalty to his identity not just as an Israelite but as a separated or consecrated Hebrew (Judg 13). As described in the story of Samson (Judg 14–16), Samson is atypical. Lawrence Stager, whose archaeological work in Ashkelon, Israel, made a significant contribution to the understanding of Philistine culture, concludes that Samson "does not fit the mold of a typical Biblical Judge of the period, nor is he a leader of Israelite armies like the other judges. He is instead an individual champion about whom many a tale was told."[24] His physical strength, his secret powers, his telling of riddles, his rage, and his revenge all have parallels in Greek mythology. Samson lives on

23. "Jew and Greek" will become a central division in the Greek New Testament. With their contrasting cultures, religions, diets, and behavior, "Jew and Greek" can be seen as another way of referring to landlubbers and seafarers.

24. See Stager, "When Canaanites and Philistines Ruled Ashkelon," 40–42.

the border between land and sea cultures, where economic, social, and cultural exchange between Philistines and Israelites occurs easily. Samson, having long ago lost his fidelity to the constraints of his Israelite identity, tragically ends his life as a prisoner in the seaport of Gaza, where he commits his last act of revenge.

The threat of the Philistines is not diminished by Samson's act of suicidal terror. In the wake of Samson's death, Israel's internal disintegration, graphically described in a series of atrocities in the final chapters of Judges, continues.[25] The people of the Land eventually become disillusioned with their method of combating the Philistines' powerful military and relentless cultural pressure. With its insistence on becoming "like other nations" in desiring a king (1 Sam 8:5), Israel seems to believe that a king will give them calculable advantages against the Philistines. But it takes more than political reform to defeat Israel's enemies. Saul's reign ends with the Philistines winning a decisive battle on Mount Gilboa, deep in Israelite territory, and brutally murdering Saul and his son Jonathan (1 Sam 31).

David

The famous story of the young David's single-handed defeat of the Philistine hero Goliath makes him the popular new hero, radically different from Samson. David is from the hill country, a shepherd, which by definition is about as far from a hero figure as a seafaring Philistine hero could ever get. Goliath is an example of a Greek warrior hero facing down a Hebrew fighter from the hills. Each embodies the different strategies of his respective sea and land fighting culture.

With David's incredible victory over the Philistine hero, the relationship between the Philistines and the Israelites begins to change. David, who is gifted in so many ways, including his ability to build

---

25. These include flagrant idolatry, all-night gang rape of a concubine that left her dead, dismemberment of the concubine with her body parts sent to the other tribes, inter-tribal war against the tribe of Benjamin at Gibeah, the slaughter of women and children, and more violence and abduction of other women to supply the Benjaminites with wives after theirs were killed in the inter-tribal violence (Judg 19–21).

strategic relationships with his cunning, charm, and reputation, uses Philistines to achieve his ambitions (1 Sam 21:10) and eventually, as king, to include Philistines in his army (2 Sam 18:2)![26]

The causes for the decline and disappearance of the once-proud Philistines are not completely clear. Unlike the isolationist land-dwelling Hebrews, the Philistine seafarer mentality allowed and motivated them to adapt, assimilate, make alliances, and intermarry with Canaanites, Phoenicians, and even Israelites. The prophets had predicted their demise, and they disappeared with the Babylonian conquest, leaving little behind except their mostly malevolent reputation derived from Hebrew Scriptures, some striking archaeological evidence of their sophistication, and their name.

THE PHOENICIANS

We now look at a far more impressive and long-lasting sea-oriented neighbor of landlocked Israelites—the Phoenicians. The Phoenicians, based on the rugged coast of what is today Lebanon, dominated shipping in the Mediterranean for over one thousand years. Seán McGrail describes the ascendancy of Phoenician seafaring: "Around 2000 BC, a number of city-states emerged on the Levant coast. The inhabitants became active in maritime trade. ... These seafaring people subsequently came to be called 'Phoenicians' by the Greeks."[27] Their trading network included the wealthy islands and port cities as well as minor trading partners like Israel, which traded their agricultural products for goods and materials from around the Mediterranean. Unlike the Philistines, their migration was from land to sea, where they quickly adapted to the opportunities provided by the rugged coastland with

26. This building of relationships between the Gittites—inhabitants of Gath, Goliath's hometown—and David is complex and limited in its details. The reason to include it here is to give some evidence at the beginning of this study that the sea and its people contributed to the change in Israelite culture and thus helped shape the Hebrew Scriptures.

27. Seán McGrail, *Boats of the World: From the Stone Age to Medieval Times* (Oxford: Oxford University Press, 2001), 128. For a thorough discussion of the Phoenician achievements of seafaring and shipbuilding, see pages 128–34.

FIGURE 5: **Harbor remains in today's Lebanon**

its ideal harbors. Their sea trading skills are legendary both in history and in Hebrew Scriptures.

Tyre was one of the city-states established by the Phoenicians by at least 2000 BC. Originally an island, just off the coast, and located about fifty miles (80 km) south of modern Beirut, it grew to become a leading trading seaport on the eastern end of the Mediterranean. So dominant was Tyre-based shipping and trade that the Mediterranean was known, along with other names, as the "Tyrian Sea." The geographical advantage of having good natural harbors, compared to the sandy beaches of the Israelite and the Philistine coastal area to the south, created an opportunity for trade connections and the development of language, products, and technology. They developed the rare and expensive purple dye manufacturing.[28]

28. The manufacturing of the famous purple or blue dye from the sea, murex shells, and market domination by the Phoenicians, is one of those extraordinary wealth-producing enterprises of history. Not only does the name "Phoenician" derive from the color purple, the eventual demand for the beautiful, permanent dye sought after by the royalty and elite of Rome on one hand, and by the religious Israelites to fulfill the requirement for the phylacteries on the other, the dye provided wealth to the Phoenicians and political connections around the Mediterranean Sea. For an intriguing investigation of the history and importance of the authentic purple dye, see Baruch Sternman, *The Rarest Blue: The Remarkable Story of an Ancient Color Lost to History and Rediscovered*, 2nd ed. (Jerusalem: Ptil Tekhelet, 2017). The author helped discover

King Solomon famously established ties with Hiram the Phoenician. Passing references to the role of the sea in transportation are contained in Kings and Chronicles. When Solomon requested Hiram king of Tyre to send him cedars from Lebanon for the building of the temple he planned to undertake in Jerusalem and offered in exchange to send Hiram a considerable annual supply of wheat and oil, Hiram's response was positive. "Hiram sent word to Solomon, 'I have heard the message that you have sent to me; I will fulfill all your needs in the matter of cedar and cypress timber. My servants shall bring it down to the sea from the Lebanon; I will make it into rafts to go by sea to the place you indicate. I will have them broken up there for you to take away. And you shall meet my needs by providing food for my household.' So Hiram supplied Solomon's every need for timber of cedar and cypress" (1 Kgs 5:8–10).

With the cooperation between King Solomon and Hiram of Tyre, the economic and political benefits of participation in trade in the Mediterranean were apparent to those who were not troubled or restricted by the perils of compromise. However, the guardians of the faith recognized the very real dangers of close and beneficial connections with the Phoenicians. Blurring the distinct identity of the people of Israel would inevitably lead to the loss of fidelity to the God of Israel alone.

THE WRITINGS AND THE PROPHETS

Different perspectives between those who benefited from the sea and its people and those who did not are apparent in the Hebrew Scriptures, which begin to include more positive references to the sea

---

the long-lost formula of production, and revived the market for the blue thread (תְּכֵלֶת, *təkēlet*) required in the Law for the garments (צִיצִת, *ṣîṣit*) of the children of Israel (Num 15:38). The discovery of an ancient major purple dye manufacturing center in Tel Shiqmona, located on the seacoast near Haifa, Israel, demonstrates the eventual extent of the economic connections between Phoenician and Israelite purple trade following Solomon's alliance with Hiram. See Golan Shalvi and Ayelet Gilboa, "Between Israel and Phoenicia: The Iron IIA-B Fortified Purple-Dye Production Centre at Tel Shiqmona," *Tel Aviv* 50 (2023): 75–110, https://doi.org/10.1080/03344355.2023.2190283.

and its people, as well as warnings by the prophets about the peril of closer connections. The Psalms, for instance, contain both judgments against "the ships of Tarshish" (48:7) and a far more accepting description of seafarers and seafaring that implies Jewish participation in sailing: "Some went down to the sea in ships, doing business on the mighty waters" (107:23). Here there is no condemnation of this participation in seafaring but praise to the Lord who controls the sea and brings his people "to their desired haven." Back on land, the seafarers "thank the LORD for his steadfast love, ... in the congregation of the people" (107:31–32). Two lengthy and detailed descriptions of the connections between seafarers and landlubbers demonstrate both the promises and perils of these connections.

THE TYRE SHIPWRECK

The warnings of these sea connections become most apparent in the writings of the prophets, especially with Ezekiel, who describes the success and judgment of Tyre so vividly. As the ship of Tyre sinks, everyone who traded with that great seaport, including Israelites, watches on in anguish as they see their prosperity going down with the ship. "Your riches, your wares, your merchandise, ... sink into the heart of the seas on the day of your ruin. ... The mariners and all the pilots of the sea stand on the shore and wail aloud over you, and cry bitterly" (Ezek 27:27, 29–30). Tyre's trade had "satisfied many peoples; with your abundant wealth and merchandise you enriched the kings of the earth" (Ezek 27:33). Solomon, who achieved wealth and power, was one of the kings who were enriched.

The story of Jezebel, the Phoenician married to King Ahab, is a dramatic demonstration of the perils of political and economic cooperation between the people of Israel and the people of the Mediterranean Sea. The story of the decline of the Northern Kingdom has begun. Israel is sinking along with Tyre.

Another story about actual Phoenician ships sinking needs to be included here. In 1997 two iron-age ships from around the eighth century BC were discovered in about four hundred feet (122 m) of water off the coast of Ashkelon. The renowned marine archaeologist Lawrence Stager oversaw a team of divers to explore and analyze the remarkable, rare remains of the ships. After twenty-eight hundred years, the ships themselves had completely disintegrated. But the cargo they were carrying, especially the pottery shipping containers called amphorae, had survived, allowing the researchers to identify many of the products the ships had been transporting.[29]

The Phoenicians were expanding their network of colonies around the Mediterranean toward the end of the eighth century BC. The two ships, named the *Tanit* and the *Elissa* by the archaeological team, could have been sailing from Tyre, or perhaps Tarshish, heading toward the northern coast of Africa. "The two shipwrecks we surveyed were loaded with amphoras once filled with wine, more than ten tons per ship. ... Ezekiel's famous oracle comparing the city of Tyre to a magnificent ship (chapter 27) [is] an account with all the credibility of an eyewitness."[30] From a careful analysis of the type of amphorae and their contents, the archaeological team concluded that the "Tanit and the Elissa were, then, ships manned by Phoenician crews and mainly loaded with a single commodity, fine wines from elsewhere decanted into and transported abroad in Phoenician amphoras."[31] Remarkable as well is how they appear to have sunk. The evidence indicates that an unexpected east wind from the desert swept the ships off course when they flooded and foundered. This is the cruel east wind (רוּחַ הַקָּדִים, *rûaḥ haqqādîm*), which sank Ezekiel's "Ship of Tyre" (Ezek 27:26), and by which, the Psalmist says, the Lord "shatters the ships of Tarshish" (Ps 48:7).[32]

For traders, shipwrecks are always incredible catastrophes. In this prophecy of Ezekiel, the voices of the traders and seafarers are heard

29. For a detailed analysis by the archaeologists and their conclusions about the Phoenicians based on the *Tanit* and the *Elissa*, see Robert D. Ballard et al., "Iron Age Shipwrecks in Deep Water off Ashkelon, Israel," *American Journal of Archaeology* 106.2 (2002): 151–68.

30. Ballard et al., "Iron Age Shipwrecks," 166.

31. Ballard et al., "Iron Age Shipwrecks," 166.

32. Ballard et al., "Iron Age Shipwrecks," 166.

more clearly than in any other biblical sea tale. Ezekiel captures the significance of the loss, the mourning, the weeping, and the wailing by everyone who benefited.

How did Ezekiel, the landlubber Hebrew prophet, get such accurate information about the extent of the trade, the variety of cargo, and the arrogance of the traders? Could it be that the traders and sea workers who connected with the people of the Land of Israel had boasted constantly about their superiority? This is highly likely.

JONAH AND THE GODS OF THE SEAS

With its details of well-meaning but terrified long-distance sailors, a man-eating fish/whale/sea monster, and a renegade prophet, all converging on a large "ship of Tarshish" in a Mediterranean storm, this story is the favorite of children and their parents everywhere, even in Nazareth. Jesus refers to the story of Jonah more times than to the stories of any other prophet of Israel. It is the perfect storm for making a point.

At the time of Jonah, during the eighth century BC, Joppa is used by the Phoenicians as well as the Canaanites and Egyptians before them, and the Assyrians, Babylonians, Persians, and Greeks after them, as a lucrative shipping port. Joppa is where world history and biblical drama happen. Situated on the *Via Maris* that links Joppa to the spice routes of the Nabatean traders from the Arabian Peninsula to the southeast and the silk route to Asia to the northeast, Joppa is a port that opens the land routes to the lucrative markets of the Mediterranean, all the way to the ends of the earth, to Tarshish, likely near the modern Strait of Gibraltar. The ships of Tarshish are legendary long-distance cargo ships of antiquity. The crew is tough and experienced. And heading west from Joppa, if they are from Tarshish, they are without a doubt eager to return home after months away.[33]

---

33. Barry Beitzel makes the case "that there existed on the Mediterranean Sea an Iron Age site or sites known outside the Bible by Phoenicians, Assyrians, and possibly by Canaanites as 'Tarshish,' which was occupied on at least one occasion by Phoenicians and that early Phoenicians were navigating a broad sweep of the Mediterranean by the tenth

We know more about Jonah. He is likely a landlubber who has never sailed the Mediterranean in his life. He is a prophet of God but shares none of God's concern for the hated Assyrian enemies, whose ambitions of expanding their empire threatened their little neighbors. To represent God's message to the inhabitants of the huge, powerful city of Nineveh is inconceivable. "Let them go to hell!" Jonah weighs the risks and concludes that he will not go.

What is Jonah thinking, contemplating the risks of disobeying a direct order from God? But wait, God is the God of the Land. The sea is the realm of the sea gods. While the sea and its gods are terrifying, going to Nineveh is inconceivable. He will take his chances on the sea where God is not, on a ship going farther from the Land and the God of the Land than any other possible destination.

The Hebrew prophet, with his bushy beard, dusty sandals, and shepherd's clothes, is spotted by the sailors. They do not pick up many Israelite passengers on their way to Tarshish. But the sailors are tough, seasoned, and eager to get back home. They have seen everything in their usually miserable and potentially short lives—the brutality of authorities, the fury of gods with their unpredictable storms, sea monsters, runaways of all kinds, slaves, criminals, prophets, and prostitutes. They know better than to question the captain or cause any delay. They respect and sometimes fear the sea. But they are courageous. They identify and relate to desperate and courageous men. They will do their best to save this Hebrew man's life. There is honor among seafarers. And maybe the gods are keeping score.

So on a very calm day, with a light northeast wind blowing, the crew members offer their sacrifices to the gods of the sea, asking for fair winds and following seas and a safe and quick return voyage to

century B.C." Barry J. Beitzel, "Was There a Joint Nautical Venture on the Mediterranean Sea by Tyrian Phoenicians and Early Israelites?" *Bulletin of the American Schools of Oriental Research* 360 (2010): 37–66. The article discusses the likelihood that the ships of Tarshish are these ships, as well as the connections of Solomon to the trade of the Phoenicians, as historically plausible. The ships had to be well built, as the distance from Joppa to the possible location of Tarshish (in present-day southern Spain) is approximately twenty-five hundred miles (4,000 km) and according to estimates could have taken up to one year to make the trip west.

Tarshish. Then with the promising wind filling its square sails, the proud ship of Tarshish departs Joppa, heading west toward Tarshish, toward home.

The story of Jonah's rescue by the "large fish" (דָּג גָּדוֹל, *dāg gādôl*) that "the LORD provided" (Jonah 1:17) is another dramatic example of God's presence in and control of the seas and everything in them.[34] The simultaneous peril of the storm and sea and God's control of both the weather and the creature of the sea are further evidence of the dual perspective of the sea by the Hebrew writers of Scripture.

SUMMARY

From creation onward, the seas are bounded waters that have been divided from both unbounded waters and land. The Hebrew Scriptures regard water/waters before and after creation to be chaotic, unpredictable, and dangerous. God alone is in control of the waters and can, like the pagan gods of the sea, calm the waters and protect his people or bring judgment on humanity, including Israel's enemies, with the waters. These divisions are positive.

The God of creation, who is the ruler of land and sea, becomes increasingly associated with the Land and its people in the Hebrew Scriptures. The sea themes of the Hebrew Scriptures are primarily about two seas. The Red Sea is mentioned twenty-eight times by name in Hebrew Scripture, more than any other named sea. God's power and absolute control of the sea are depicted and celebrated in the story. The memory of the Red Sea event is only negative until God's mighty deliverance of the Israelites and judgment of the Egyptian pursuers

34. The identity of the creature that swallowed Jonah as a "great fish" seems to indicate how unfamiliar Jonah was with the creatures of the sea or the possibility that he did not see the creature clearly except for the gaping mouth. In any case, there is some ambiguity in the creature's identity in the story. Jesus, in telling the story of Jonah, calls the creature a κῆτος (*kētos*), translated in the NRSV as "sea monster" (Matt 12:40). The word used in Greek implies the fish has a gaping mouth. The word is translated as "whale" in some versions of the Greek New Testament. Job uses the Hebrew word תַּנִּין (*tannîn*) variously translated as "whale" or "dragon." To add further to the ambiguity and possibilities, sailing over a three-year period on the likely route between Joppa and the eastern end of the Mediterranean, I was delighted on two different occasions at early dawn to witness a very large solitary whale blowing and fluking (diving).

occurs. Then the memory is positive. The recounting of God's miraculous deliverance of the Hebrews and his judgment of the Egyptians at the Red Sea in the past and the descriptions of the recurring threats and promises of the Mediterranean Sea in the present run through the entire Hebrew Scriptures.

The Israelite encounters with their seafaring neighbors shape their perspective toward the Mediterranean Sea and the rest of the world. What they learn of the sea and its peoples is from the ones who arrive by ship to the Land. Knowledge of the sea invaders' places of origin is limited in Hebrew Scripture. But as they develop closer connections with Mediterranean seafarers, the geography of the Mediterranean becomes more specific in the Hebrew Scriptures. For instance, the Hebrew word אִי (ʾî), variously translated as "islands" or "coastlands," is used thirty-seven times in Hebrew Scripture and is generally a vague reference to islands or coastlands, associated with the "ends of the earth." The coastlands and islands are distant, strange, evil, dangerous, and unseen places. But in later writings, the sea-invading Philistines are identified as coming from a specific island with a name—Caphtor or Crete (Jer 47:4).

The perspectives on the sea from the Writings and the Prophets in the Hebrew Scriptures begin to evolve as the relationships of the Israelites with their seafaring neighbors improve. But while political and trading alliances solidified by marriage bring apparent economic advantages and political stability, there are risks. The prophets point out that maintaining cultural isolation is necessary for protecting Israelite identity and commitment to God from the perils of the sea and its people. At the same time, improving connections to the rest of the world via the sea and its people is seen by political and religious leaders of Israel as potentially having political and economic benefits. King David and especially King Solomon recognize the potential of connections to the sea and its people.

Then, as the kingdom is divided between Israel and Judah, some kings of Israel continue to further develop cooperative relationships with their Phoenician neighbors directly to the north, something strenuously opposed by the Hebrew prophets. The prophet Elijah's confrontation with King Ahab and his loyalists on Mount Carmel (1 Kgs 18:17–46) demonstrates Israel's concurrent positive and negative views of the sea and its people within the Hebrew texts.

But a third view emerges among the Prophets—a time of universal peace and blessing, with all nations of both land and sea participating in the promises of God together.[35] This third view of the potential of the sea and its people will shape the story in the Greek New Testament.

THE CHANGING TIDE

Hebrew Scripture ends with the sea being described in terms of both judgment and hope borne by the sea. The Greek and Roman military and cultural triumph over the inhabitants of the Mediterranean basin brings new intensity to both the peril and the potential to the people of the Land. The options for the people of Israel, ranging between accommodation and resistance, are reflected in the writings of the Apocrypha and the New Testament. So extensive will be the Greek impact on the people of Israel that Greek will be the primary language in which the rest of Jewish Scriptures will be written. The accommodation by the people of the Land to the language of the people living around the Mediterranean Sea allows for growing opportunities and benefits of cultural exchange along with unprecedented threats to religious and national identity. Accommodation or resistance among the various factions in Israel increases the tension between the powerful, the wealthy, and the esteemed and those who are excluded from these "blessings." The tide for the people of the Land is rising—a cultural flood tide.

With the maximum difference between high and low tides on the shores of the eastern end of the Mediterranean Sea today averaging

35. The prophet Isaiah especially foresees and describes this era of universal peace and blessing in Isaiah 11.

only about one foot, tides are barely even noticed. The changing cultural tide from land to sea apparent in Hebrew Scripture is also easy to overlook. While the shift may be gradual and barely noticeable, the change begins to expose some fissures below the surface of the Israelites' ebbing and flowing attitudes toward the sea and its people. It becomes a "sea change" shaping Scripture itself and is the focus of the following chapters of this study.

REFLECTIONS FROM THE SEA

We spent our first winter in the Ashkelon Marina in Israel. We had decided on Ashkelon because it was the farthest south (and warmest), it was beautiful, and, because of its proximity to Gaza, it was very affordable. Ashkelon was to be our home for the next six months. What a community! Local Israelis, sailors from around the world, fishermen.

Years before, Janet and I had spent a year living in Jerusalem. From the moment we arrived in Ashkelon, it was obvious, especially on Shabbat (the Sabbath) when the locals from Tel Aviv and other areas along the coast would come to eat, drink, and frolic on the beach, that we were not in Jerusalem.

One Shabbat a boating neighbor couple, Jewish sailors from Russia who had a car, invited us to go with them to a large grocery store. "You can shop on Shabbat?" I asked incredulously. "Sure, why not?" they responded. So off we went. The place was humming. The selections were stunning. And then I found it: pork chops! I could not believe this—riding in a car to go shopping for pork on Shabbat in Israel.

But this was Ashkelon, on the sea, where rabbinic interpretation of Sabbath law had little traction in the marina. Ashkelon remains, in our experience, a Philistine city. Their sea culture has been embraced by the people of the Land. The prophets of Jerusalem still do not approve. We learned to love them all, Philistine and Israelite, Sea and Land, Ashkelon and Jerusalem.

CHAPTER 2

PERILS: THE MEDITERRANEAN SEA FROM HEBREW TO GREEK SCRIPTURES

"They that sail upon the seas tell of the danger thereof; and when we hear it with our ears, we marvel thereat."
Sirach 43:24 (KJV)

THE GREAT SEA

There is no "Mediterranean Sea" in Scripture. It is mostly the "Great Sea" in the Bible.[1] The name "Mediterranean Sea" did not come until long after both the Hebrew and Greek Scriptures were written. However, the Mediterranean, although comprising less than one percent of the world's ocean areas, looms large in both Scripture

1. This most common Hebrew usage of either "the Sea" or the "Great Sea" (הַיָּם הַגָּדוֹל, *hayyām haggādôl*) when referring to what is later named the "Mediterranean Sea" parallels the references used by many others in ancient texts. In Greek, it is simply "the Sea" (ἡ θάλασσα, *hē thalassa*) or sometimes "the Great Sea" (ἡ μεγάλη θάλασσα, *hē megalē thalassa*). The Latin name used by the Romans before their empire was "Great Sea" (*mare magnum*) or "Internal Sea" (*mare internum*). Phoenician ancient texts use "the Great Sea."

and Western history.[2] The Israelite inhabitants of the Land, until the Roman domination of the sea, usually called the Mediterranean Sea "the Great Sea," sometimes the "Western Sea," for it was specified as the westernmost boundary of the Land. But in general, the Mediterranean, as previously noted, was called by many names by the people who lived around it; the most common one was simply "Sea." For the ancient writers, there was no other sea to which so many people had such access, or which had such an impact in their history. The "Sea" in the Jewish experience in the Land was the only sea that mattered.

Here I must include a personal admission of bias. What began in 2004 as a fifteen-month sailing sabbatical in the Mediterranean following the sea routes of the apostle Paul turned into a twenty-year fascination with this most intriguing sea of our planet. Historically, culturally, religiously, politically, economically, and geographically, there is simply no other body of water in human history that has played such a gigantic role in birthing Western civilization and thus impacted the entire world. Although tiny in comparison to other seas, the Mediterranean is at once the cradle of civilization. It is also the cradle (and the graveyard) of two powerful thalassocracies—the sea-based empires of Scripture—that we will be tracing. The Greeks, mentioned in the Apocrypha, were the first of the true thalassocracies to invade Judea, followed by the Roman Empire of the New Testament Scriptures—the biggest and best empire ever to rule the Mediterranean so successfully for so long. The fascination with the Mediterranean Sea shared by historians, biblical scholars, and seafarers from antiquity to the present is well deserved.

Although the Mediterranean Sea is tiny as far as seas go, it is the largest inland sea on the planet. The length, measuring from the Strait of Gibraltar at the western mouth, to the Atlantic Ocean, to Israel on the eastern end in the Levant, is a mere 2,500 miles (4,000 km).

---

2. There is an excellent body of literature on the geographical features of the Mediterranean Sea. For a summary of its physical features, see Oliver Rackham, "The Physical Setting," in *The Mediterranean in History*, ed. David Abulafia (London: Thames and Hudson, 2003), 33–65.

The greatest distance from the north (Croatia) to the south (Libya) is just over 1,400 miles (2,273 km), with the average width from north to south being about 500 miles (800 km). The average depth of the Mediterranean Sea is 4,900 feet (1,500 m), with the deepest point measured as 16,762 feet (5,109 m).

All of the rivers, and the Black Sea, flowing constantly *into* the Mediterranean Sea are not sufficient to offset the rapid rate of evaporation. The Mediterranean Sea level is maintained by the constant inflow of the Atlantic Ocean through the relatively shallow and narrow Strait of Gibraltar, the famous "Pillars of Hercules." Being almost landlocked, the Mediterranean Sea lacks strong currents and massive tidal variation, which limits the exchange of water. This affects the salinity; the levels of plankton and other organic matter, which give the Mediterranean its characteristic deep blue water; and, of course, the quantity of marine life. The deep blue, sparkling waters of the Mediterranean are legendary. Homer uses the term "wine-dark sea" (οἶνοψ πόντος, *oinops pontos*) in the *Odyssey* (e.g., book 5, line 132), the interpretation of which is a subject of much debate, and this is even the title of Thomas Cahill's popular book on Greek history and culture.[3] The phenomenal clarity and blue coloration are because, according to marine biologists, "the vivid blue waters of the Mediterranean Sea reflect the very low biomass of phytoplankton (the 'grass' of the world's oceans) making it as much a desert as the Sahara to the south."[4]

And then there is the weather. The unpredictable and challenging weather is legendary from antiquity to today.[5] "Sailing conditions in

3. Thomas Cahill, *Sailing the Wine-Dark Sea: Why the Greeks Matter* (New York: Anchor Books, 2004).

4. Helen R. Powley et al., "Nutrient Cycling in the Mediterranean Sea: The Key to Understanding How the Unique Marine Ecosystem Functions and Responds to Anthropogenic Pressures," in *Mediterranean Identities: Environment, Society, Culture*, ed. Borna Fuerst-Bjeliš (London: IntechOpen, 2017), 48, https://doi.org/10.5772/intechopen.70878.

5. The shipwreck story in Acts 27 is the best example. However, it is not only the long late-season storm that caused Paul's ship to run aground on Malta; the entire westward voyage to Rome was extremely challenging—and accurate. "We sailed slowly for a number of days and arrived with difficulty off Cnidus, ... as the wind was against us" (Acts 27:7). I have sailed

the Mediterranean have been reviled and ridiculed by modern sailors more than in any other part of the world and the most repeated saying is that 'in the Mediterranean one either gets too much wind or none at all and what one gets is on the nose.'"[6] The terrifying accounts of storms and shipwrecks abound in ancient texts, including in Scripture.

For such a small body of water, the Mediterranean Sea has a surprisingly long coastline, thanks to the sheer number of islands and the ruggedness of the northern coast. While 28,600 miles (46,000 km) is impressive, it is the sheer number of radically different countries sharing the coastline that makes the Mediterranean so unique. This small sea connects three continents within easy sailing distance: Europe, Asia, and Africa. Living around this sea is an incredibly diverse collection of humanity of biblical proportions "from every nation [ἔθνος, *ethnos*], from all tribes and peoples and languages" (Rev 7:9). Indeed, during the first century AD, in addition to both Latin and Greek, a bewildering variety of languages was spoken by people of different regions and ethnicities. Socrates famously describes it: "We inhabit a small portion of the earth ... living round the sea like ... frogs round a pond."[7]

A total of twenty-two countries, two of which are island countries, and one territory, on three continents, share the Mediterranean![8] In addition, there are around 250 inhabited islands out of 3,300 islands in the Mediterranean. These islands, ranging from a population of five on Marathi, Greece, to Sicily's over five million inhabitants, all

---

that exact same route many times, and to this day, the wind around Cnidus, when it blows, is almost always exactly as Luke describes it in Acts.

6. Jimmy Cornell, *World Cruising Routes*, 4th ed. (Camden, ME: International Marine, 1998), 532.

7. Plato, *Phaedo*, 109B (trans. Hugh Tredennick, *The Last Days of Socrates* [London: Penguin Books, 1954]).

8. Beginning at the northwest and moving clockwise, these are: Spain, France, Monaco, Italy, Slovenia, Croatia, Bosnia and Herzegovina, Montenegro, Albania, Greece, Turkey, Syria, Lebanon, Israel, Palestine, Egypt, Libya, Tunisia, Algeria, and Morocco. Malta and Cyprus are island countries in the sea. Gibraltar is an overseas territory of the United Kingdom. From earliest recorded history until today, the people sharing the Mediterranean have cooperated and clashed. The fact that Rome was the only empire in history to have integrated the entire diverse population into a single entity will be examined below.

make their distinct contributions to the diverse cohesiveness of the Mediterranean.[9] The late prominent French historian of the Mediterranean Fernand Braudel describes the significance of the Mediterranean:

> It is in fact the major feature of the sea's destiny that it should be locked inside the largest group of landmasses on the globe, the "gigantic linked continent" of Europe-Asia-Africa, a sort of planet in itself, where goods and people circulated from the earliest times. Human beings found a theater for their historical drama in these three conjoined continents. This was where crucial exchanges took place.
>
> And since this human history was in perpetual motion, flowing down to the shore of the Mediterranean where it regularly came to a halt, is it any wonder that the sea should so soon have become one of the living centers of the universe?[10]

Braudel identifies two major features of the Mediterranean Sea as "the unity and the coherence of the Mediterranean region ... and the ... greatness of the Mediterranean."[11]

THE GREAT SEA IN HEBREW SCRIPTURE

The first mention of what is now called the Mediterranean Sea in Hebrew Scripture appears in Joshua 1:4, defining the extent of the territory promised by God as "all the land of the Hittites to the Great Sea" (*hayyām haggādôl*). An earlier reference (Exod 23:31) refers to the Mediterranean Sea as the "sea of the Philistines" (יָם פְּלִשְׁתִּים, *yām*

9. Based on interviews with inhabitants of more than thirty islands and participant observation of social events, informal interactions, and social patterns, I have concluded that islanders, in addition to sharing an intense sense of their island identity, feel at once more isolated and more connected than communities on the mainland. I will return to the key role played by islands in the Roman maritime system in chapter 4.

10. Fernand Braudel, *Memory and the Mediterranean* (New York: Knopf, 2001), 15–16.

11. Fernand Braudel, *The Mediterranean and the Mediterranean World in the Age of Philip II*, trans. Siân Reynolds (New York: Harper & Row, 1972), 14.

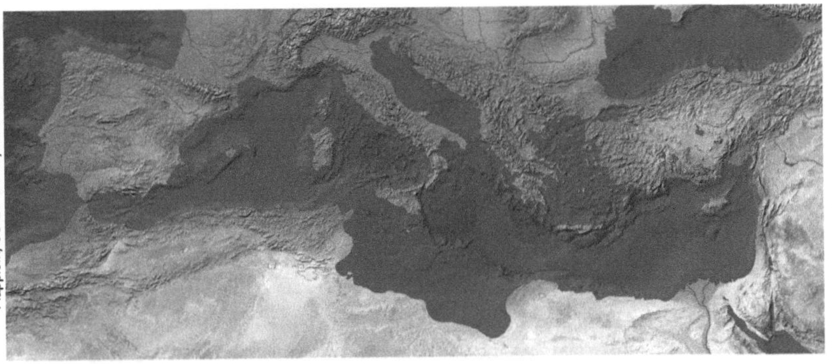

MAP 1: **The Great Sea**

pəlištîm), but this is likely referring to the coastal area of Philistine territory rather than the entire Mediterranean.

As mentioned in the previous chapter, the growing familiarity with the features of the Mediterranean Sea and the seafaring people as the Hebrews encounter them is evident in Scripture. Initially, however, their knowledge of the sea, based as it is on their experience of their seafaring enemies, is quite limited. For instance, after the account of Noah building the ark in Genesis, "the only biblical passage in which shipbuilding is mentioned is found in 1 Kings 9:26–27."[12] The powerful description of seafaring in the Psalms (107:23–32), however, clearly demonstrates a growing familiarity with the sea.

It is within this framework of their connections that the perspective on the sea and its people expands and develops in the Hebrew Scripture and the geography of the lands around the Mediterranean becomes more specific. As the people of the Land of Israel connect increasingly to the people of the sea, both willingly and unwillingly, the land-based perspective that shapes the Hebrew Scriptures will be challenged as the cultural, linguistic, political, and economic power of the Greeks, the ultimate sea people, comes ashore.

12. Raphael Patai, *Children of Noah: Jewish Seafaring in Ancient Times* (Princeton, NJ: Princeton University Press, 1998), 12. Patai also mentions Jehoshaphat's attempt to build "Tarshish ships" (1 Kgs 22:48–49; Patai, *Children of Noah*, 13).

The Greeks are the Mediterranean seafarers par excellence. The apocryphal writings, written mostly in Greek, demonstrate the threat of the first thalassocracy (seaborne empire) faced by the people of the Land of Israel. The seafaring Greeks threatened the people living in the Land not only militarily but also culturally, as they did everywhere they went. So successful were the Greeks that virtually all of the major seaports around the entire rim of the Mediterranean incorporated features of Greek culture.

The Greek seafaring people, who challenged the Phoenicians for control of the Mediterranean trade, had immigrated to the coastal areas from their inland origins, like the Phoenicians themselves.[13] Like other groups of migrants from land to sea, they had learned to adapt and take advantage of the geographic features of their shoreline. The rugged seacoasts of both Phoenicia (modern Lebanon) and Greece, with their many natural harbors, made seafaring accessible for many inhabitants. Because of their proximity to and intimate familiarity with the sea, they were also acutely aware of the capricious nature of the sea and in awe of its power. Salvatore Cosentino notes, "People were afraid of the sea because of its marked unpredictability, which constantly exposes ships and mariners to the risks of tempests. Whereas living on land provides men with a rhythm of existence much more predictable and realizable, the sea is an untrustworthy environment."[14]

Yet the lure of the sea was irresistible, and a kind of deep, almost romantic relationship toward the sea developed to the extent that the Greeks and their sea became inseparable in history. The Attic vases depict all kinds of sea-related scenes. Such an abundance of depictions would have been impossible without an intimate relationship with the sea. Cosentino explains:

---

13. For an overview of the close relationship of the Greeks with the sea, see Salvatore Cosentino, "Mentality, Technology and Commerce: Shipping amongst the Mediterranean Islands in Late Antiquity and Beyond," in *The Insular System of the Early Byzantine Mediterranean*, ed. Demetrios Michaelides, Philippe Pergola, and Enrico Zanini, British Archaeological Reports International Series 2523 (Oxford: Archaeopress, 2013), 65–76.

14. Cosentino, "Mentality," 65.

> The Greeks prided themselves in this relationship, enjoyed the sea and activity on it from fishing, relaxing and frequenting among other floating businesses, brothel boats. [The Greeks] saw themselves as distinct from others such as the land-based Persians, who, while utilizing the sea for their expansive purposes, were not really at home the way the Greeks were.[15]

Neither were the Israelites at home on the sea.

But seafaring in the Mediterranean, because it could be so lucrative, had always been fiercely competitive. Following an earlier period of decline in Greek seafaring due to rampant piracy and Phoenician control of trade, the seafaring Greeks began to ascend again. Lionel Casson describes the emerging Greek competition of Phoenician trade—"While Phoenicia was sailing the eastern and western Mediterranean with a completely free hand, the Greek world was emerging. ... By 800 BC it had by and large taken the shape it was to have in its heyday three centuries later."[16] By forming a cooperative network among independent cities of the Greek peninsula; the major islands of Crete, Rhodes, and Cyprus; and cities scattered along the southern coast of Asia Minor, Greek ships "once again plied the sea in great numbers. The time was right for Greece to embark on its own program of colonization."[17]

A period of conquest and the creation of new Greek settlements followed, challenging and changing all of the local cultures. "The Greeks, between 750 and 550 BC, in a series of concerted bursts of activity, settled themselves the length and breadth of the Mediterranean. ... They founded in the neighborhood of 250 colonies, a number of which have had a continuous existence ever since. ... In a very real sense, the boatloads of Greeks that crossed the sea in those two centuries were the advance guard of Western civilization."[18]

---

15. Cosentino, "Mentality," 65.

16. Lionel Casson, *The Ancient Mariners: Seafarers and Sea Fighters of the Mediterranean in Ancient Times*, 2nd ed. (Princeton, NJ: Princeton University Press, 1991), 66.

17. Casson, *Ancient Mariners*, 66.

18. Casson, *Ancient Mariners*, 67.

With the triumph of the Greeks over the Persians in a fierce naval battle in 480 and the land battle of 479 BC, the first true thalassocracy in the Mediterranean would rule not only the waves but the shores of the eastern Mediterranean.[19] Persia, the last great land-based empire that had adapted to sea warfare with the help of Phoenician maritime skills, was outmatched by Greek seafaring skill and their formidable triremes.[20]

Before Alexander III ("the Great") launched his successful land campaign against the Persians in the late 330s BC and conquered the Levant shortly thereafter, the powerful armies that had invaded and occupied the Land of Israel and enslaved its people before the Greeks had been primarily from land-based empires. With the ascent of Alexander, the successful struggle eastward for control of the Mediterranean and the lands that lay beyond the eastern end quickly displaced both the beneficial and antagonistic relationships the Israelites had with their seafaring neighbors, the Phoenicians. Now it would be the Greeks who would attract and repel the Jews of the Land of Israel. The conquering Greeks would give their own name to the region—Judea.

Following Alexander's death in Babylon shortly after his conquest of the Levant (which was likely seen as God's judgment by the Jews of Judea) the struggle for succession began with armed conflict between the Seleucids and the Ptolemies for control of the Greek territories, a vast area reaching from Anatola in the northwest (modern Turkey) to the border of India, and south to the Levant (modern Syria, Lebanon, Jordan, and Israel). During that period, the region became heavily Hellenized. Tensions mounted between Greeks and locals, especially between the Greek occupiers and the Jews of Jerusalem. There would

---

19. The two famous victories that would change the fortunes of the Greeks were the naval Battle of Salamis in 480 BC and the Persian army at the Battle of Plataea in 429–427 BC.

20. Triremes were shallow draft warships, with three tiers of rowers. Nimble and equipped to ram enemy ships at water level, they were far superior to the Persian navy vessels. For a detailed description of triremes and how they were used so effectively against much larger navies, see Casson, *Ancient Mariners,* 83–96.

be no compromise between the people of the Land and the people of the sea.

The festering resentment exploded into full-scale revolt when Antiochus IV, it is believed, desecrated the temple in 167 BC by sacrificing a pig on an altar of Zeus in the temple area. This is the most dramatic demonstration of the clash between Greek cultural insensitivity and Jewish moral sensitivity. With an outrage of this proportion, the response of Mattathias Maccabeus, serving as a temple priest at the time, ignited the Maccabean Revolt. Eventually, after a bloody but successful guerrilla campaign against the superior Greek forces, independence was achieved, and the Hasmonean Kingdom was established. No longer was Judea just one of the tribal areas of inheritance, but most of the rest of the region was included in Judea.

However, as the Hasmoneans would experience, they might be able to throw the Greeks out of the Land, but it is much more difficult to erase the cultural influence of Hellenism from the hearts and minds of the people of the Land. The culture of the Greeks, shaped as it was by the embrace of the sea and carried across the sea by Greek invaders, had taken root in Judea. This cultural invasion left divisions among the people of Judea.

Israel had not faced this kind of invasive and ongoing cultural threat before. The Greeks' wisdom; their quest for excellence; their understanding of the universe; their exuberant embrace of all the possibilities of life; and their language, art, and love of all features of human life and potential were at once attractive, repulsive, or both to the Jewish people, now free from the hated Greek occupiers. Their impact was so pervasive, so adaptable, and so durable that the term "Greek" was used to designate anyone who was not Jewish, as well as for Jews who embraced aspects of Greek culture, even in Judea. The Jews of Judea adopted the Greek language. No matter what the Judeans thought of the Greeks, speaking and thinking in the language of their former occupiers made it easier to *think like Greeks.*

THE GREAT SEA IN GREEK APOCRYPHAL WRITINGS

The apocryphal writings of the Second Temple period, while not viewed by all Christian traditions as Scripture, are rich in both reinforcing the general views of the Hebrew Scriptures toward the sea and giving insight into the sea invasion of the Greek armies into the Land of Israel and the resulting impact of this powerful pagan culture on every feature of Jewish life. I will include the fifteen books as Greek Scripture, for they represent the perspective of the Jewish writers toward the sea and its people during the time between the Hebrew Scripture and the Greek New Testament.[21] Although the relationship to the sea and its people depicted in the Greek Apocrypha is essentially the same as in the Hebrew Scripture, the confrontation by and appeal of Greek language and culture take on new levels of threat. Further, opportunities increase for Jewish people willing to adapt at the risk of being accused of, and likely guilty of, compromising their distinct identity. And it is during this time that the Jewish community begins to flourish in the great Hellenistic seaports of Alexandria and Antioch.

SUMMARY COMPARISONS

The Hebrew Scriptures, despite the Jews' limited access to and experience of the Mediterranean, use the word "sea" about twenty-five percent more frequently than the Apocrypha. This is in part because references to the Red Sea appear so frequently. Twenty percent of the references to "sea" in the Hebrew Scripture are to the Red Sea. The Red Sea constitutes only about ten percent of the sea references in the Apocrypha. This is no surprise. The clear and present threat of "sea" is the Mediterranean. When the Apocrypha writers do refer to

---

21. While there are more apocryphal writings, and not all fifteen books of the Apocrypha were originally written in Greek, they were all translated into Greek and, like the Greek Septuagint, demonstrate the pervasiveness of Greek language among the Jews. This embrace of the Greek language by many Jews in the diaspora and in Judea at the time replaced Hebrew Scripture, and even the language of worship. This powerful conduit for Greek concepts and values was now embedded in the "language of the heart" of the Jewish people.

the Red Sea, it is precisely as the Hebrew writers do—a memory of God's deliverance and salvation.

The writers of the Apocrypha mention the Mediterranean Sea either literally or as a metaphor for the threat of evil, danger, and impurity a total of forty-one times, or fifty-six percent of the mentions of "sea." The Hebrew Scriptures in comparison mention the Mediterranean Sea in the same ways, but only ninety-nine times, or thirty-five percent of the "sea" mentions. While the Hebrew Scriptures and the Greek Apocrypha both mention the Red Sea and the Mediterranean Sea, for the Jewish writers of the Apocrypha it is the Mediterranean Sea of the present rather than the Red Sea of the past that gets the attention.

History and the experience of the Israelites under the Greek sea invaders again turned the tide for Israel toward negativity following a period of beneficial trade relationships developed under Solomon and the kings of Israel. By the time of the Gospels, the Mediterranean was viewed from the Land of Israel as it had been earlier—the conduit of evil. But not everyone held this view. Rome's brutal occupation of Judea on the one hand and the seduction of cooperation and compromise on the other further divided the Jewish society politically and, with the Jewish diaspora, geographically as well. This will be examined in the following chapter.

SEA TRAVEL AND HELLENIZATION

Travel in antiquity was not something one did for enjoyment. Shahnaz Habib notes the difficulties travelers encountered in premodern times:

> Famously, the word travel is etymologically related to travail, which in turn has its origins in the Latin noun *trapezium*—a three-pronged metal device that ancient Romans used to torture prisoners. Today, for us, travel is a reprieve from the travails of work and daily life. But in those early days, travel was fraught with travail. ... Roadways were infested with brigands

> while pirate ships trolled the high seas. ... Travelers could look forward to weeks and months of slow and life-threatening travel, which often meant that they were effectively severing domestic ties for the duration of their journeys.[22]

Despite the hazards of sea travel, the domination of Greek culture was occurring everywhere on the Mediterranean before Rome wrested absolute control of the sea. But as the military might of Rome increased, the movement of people on the Mediterranean reached unprecedented heights. With the flourishing of trading vessels plying the Mediterranean, sea travel had become so safe and accessible during the Greek and early Roman periods that by the first century, people could, for personal reasons such as health treatments and religious pilgrimages, or even out of ordinary curiosity, visit the famous sites where the power and triumph of kings and gods were on display.[23] The sea was key to constant human movement in the empire, and this movement reinforced and spread the worldview, ideals, and life of the Greco-Roman Mediterranean world.[24]

---

22. Shahnaz Habib, *Airplane Mode: An Irreverent History of Travel* (New York: Catapult, 2023), chap. 5, Kindle. While Habib is describing travel during medieval times, the description applies to travel, especially by sea, in antiquity, as the travel accounts in Acts demonstrate.

23. One of the best studies on ancient travel is Lionel Casson's *Travel in the Ancient World* (London: Allan & Unwin, 1974). Also, Tony Perrottet's travelogue *Pagan Holiday: On the Trail of Ancient Roman Tourists* (New York: Random House, 2003) provides an entertaining insight into the tourist industry that had begun to flourish in the Mediterranean.

24. Of the so-called "seven wonders of the ancient world," the most famous list being compiled by the historian Herodotus, all except one, the rumored Hanging Gardens of Babylon, were located around the rim of the Mediterranean, easily accessible by sea. All were demonstrations of the power and triumph of the gods, emperors, or both. Even the famous lighthouse of Alexandria at the harbor of Alexandria in Egypt, the only wonder that served a practical function, bore the inscription: "Dedicated to the Savior gods, on behalf of those who sail the seas." The Colossus of Rhodes, which may have straddled the entrance of the Mandraki Harbor on the Island of Rhodes, was dedicated to the sun god. Artemis' temple at Ephesus, another harbor city, was the center of worship for the Ephesian Artemis. The statue of Zeus at Olympia was dedicated to Zeus, the most powerful of the Greek gods. The mausoleum at Halicarnassus (the modern port city of Bodrum, Turkey) was the final resting place for a king. In addition, every major harbor around the Mediterranean was also a showcase of the power and success of the Greek culture. Temples to the gods and emperors, even in the port city of Caesarea in the Land of Israel, dominated the high ground above many harbors. Other harbors boasted spectacular temples literally at the water's edge. Monuments commemorating the achievements

The Roman general Pompey, sailing with his navy along the trade routes toward pirate strongholds on the eastern end of the Mediterranean in 67 BC, conducted a rapid, brutal, and successful campaign, defeating the pirate threat in a mere forty days. A few years later in 63 BC, Pompey invaded Judea and established Roman control over the whole region. Herod the Great arrived on the scene in 37 BC as the first "king of Judea" appointed by Rome.[25] Josephus tersely recounts his arrival: "By this time Herod had sailed out of Italy to Ptolemais [present-day Akko, or Acre], and had gotten together no small army, both of strangers and his own country-men, and marched through Galilee."[26]

It is in the era of Roman occupation of Judea that the Greek New Testament begins. Even the Sea of Galilee is being utilized for Roman purposes, but compared to the Mediterranean, with its flourishing seaports like Antioch dominating the eastern end, it is largely irrelevant. The Jewish residents of Antioch will take a leading role in the Acts story, as will Barnabas from Salamis, Cyprus. The peril of the Mediterranean is well known to the Jewish residents of Antioch, but soon, the promises of the Mediterranean will be recognized as well. But not by all. The religious leaders in Jerusalem, whether the leaders of the various parties within rabbinic Judaism or even Jewish believers in Jesus in Jerusalem, recognize the danger of the seduction of

---

of the emperors as well as shopping areas and theaters immediately adjacent to the harbors were common. The triumph of Hellenization, from the point of view of the sea traveler at the beginning of the first century BC, must have seemed complete. The Roman Empire's expansion to the eastern end of the Mediterranean and beyond must have seemed inevitable, even to many Jews living in the stubborn Roman province of Judea. With Rome, the peril of Hellenization continued to push the Jewish population toward rebellion or cooperation. The divisions were deep, passionate, and sometimes violent.

25. While Herod's genealogy, his shifting alliances, his rise to power, and his signature grandiose building projects in Judea—including the temple—are fascinating, I will only cite the sea connection of Herod the Great's successful campaign to win Rome's appointment as ruler. Herod's Galilean military campaign included the capture of Sepphoris in Galilee in 37 BC and the development of it into a beautiful Greco-Roman city. Sepphoris is around four miles (6 km) from Nazareth. The boy Jesus would likely have heard the stories of that campaign, as well as a rebellion against Rome that occurred in 4 BC, very close to the time Jesus was born.

26. Flavius Josephus, *Jewish Antiquities* 14.15.1 (trans. William Whiston, *The Works of Josephus: Complete and Unabridged* [Peabody, MA: Hendrickson, 1987]).

Hellenism and cooperation with Rome. Hellenized Jews, more open to the sea, will change the narrative of Greek Scriptures far beyond anything yet seen in both Hebrew Scripture and the Apocrypha.

REFLECTIONS FROM THE SEA

It was about two o'clock in the morning, somewhere between Turkey and Paphos, Cyprus, on the ancient Phoenician and Greek trade routes. After months of sailing the Aegean, and then along the southern coast of Turkey, we had set out from Antalya at ten in the morning bound for Paphos, Cyprus. We were heading toward the Ashkelon Marina in Israel, where we planned to spend the winter aboard *SailingActs*. We were a little uneasy, knowing that we would be crossing the shipping lane along the southern Turkish coast that had once been used by Pompey's navy heading for the Cilician pirate strongholds but was now frequented by modern container ships traveling over twenty knots.

By this time it was late September 2024. Since beginning the voyage in June we had only sailed during the daylight. And so we had more than a little anxiety as the Turkish coastline grew faint, then disappeared altogether. The sun slipped below the horizon. There was no moon. Darkness closed in. We felt, for the first time, an awesome sense of smallness on a vast expanse of black waters, alone there on the face of the deep.

Janet had ended her watch and was now sound asleep in the bunk below deck. As we were crossing a shipping lane, lights of cargo ships would appear on the horizon, then eventually disappear over the horizon. My anxiety slowly melted, although I knew we would be crossing the ancient routes still used by modern, high-speed cargo ships.

"Always keep checking from every direction, all the time, that you are not on a collision course," our sailing instructor years earlier had warned.

"Piece of cake," I congratulated myself after tracking the trajectory of a ship that had just passed by after coming uncomfortably close. But somehow, I had forgotten there might also be other ships out there. When I finally turned around, I could not believe my eyes, for seemingly bursting out of the darkness, only seconds away from smashing into *SailingActs* was the gigantic prow of a ship, so close that I could not even see the bridge or even the running lights! I froze for about three precious seconds. Should I speed up? Slow down? Try to turn out of the path?

In the fourth second, I frantically grabbed the spotlight and pointed it directly at the bow less than one hundred yards away, approaching at what appeared to be exactly a right angle. I saw two things in that instant: "MSC" in gigantic white letters on the bow, and a huge wake coming off both sides of the bow. But wait! The wake being thrown off the bow was bigger on one side than the other, and somehow, with adrenaline-assisted trigonometric instincts, I instantly recognized that the ship was coming at just enough angle to miss us. And it did, passing mere yards behind *SailingActs.*

At that moment I appreciated a little more the ambivalence of the writers of Scripture toward the sea, so attractive and tempting, so awful and terrifying. I became like a novice Hebrew psalmist, at once trembling at the encounter with the perils of the sea and its seafaring people and praising the God who saves weak and ignorant landlubbers from them.

CHAPTER 3

DOMINATION: *MARE NOSTRUM* AND THE GREEK NEW TESTAMENT

"The Mediterranean is ours because it touches all nations."
Attributed to Seneca the Younger

MARE NOSTRUM

It was the Romans who first called the Mediterranean *Mare Nostrum* (our sea). Previously they called it the *Mare Internum* (inner sea). With their successes in the Punic War with Carthage of the seafaring Phoenicians, they began, with their usual modesty, to call it *Mare Nostrum*. And, practically speaking, it was. In every case, regardless of the Roman designation, from the perspective of the Hebrew inhabitants of the Land of Promise, the sea was pagan, threatening, unclean, dangerous—a place to be avoided. The God of the Land might rule the waves, but he did not dwell there.

While the language and the culture of the Greeks permeated Mediterranean society, by the time the New Testament era began, the Romans' military control had replaced Greek hegemony as the dominant existential reality, not only in the areas the Greeks had once ruled but everywhere around the entire eastern rim of the Sea. How was this incredible achievement accomplished?

For the Israelite inhabitants of the Promised Land, the Great Sea belonged to the gentiles—it was their sea, and if they would stay out of the Promised Land, they could keep it. But the mighty seafaring expansionists throughout history and in the biblical story—Philistines, Phoenicians, Greeks, and Romans—viewed the world, themselves, and landlubbers in general entirely differently. For the powerful empires of Scripture, the sea and land belonged to those mighty enough to take it.

The Hebrew Scriptures include, as we have seen, stories *about* the strangers who sailed the seas, who worshiped sea-like gods, who intimidated and enticed the Hebrews. They flourished on the coastal areas of the Promised Land, claiming it for themselves. In the stories, these sea invaders and their gods seem to be like the sea—unstable, unclean, volatile, seductive, full of promise and peril. They interact constantly with the Hebrews in trade, politics, war, love, friendship, marriage, religion, fear, and loathing. But they do not tell their own story in the Hebrew Scriptures.

In contrast, in the Greek Scriptures, the writers themselves are seafarers. They are in the sea stories. By the time of Jesus, the connections between the seafarers and inhabitants of the Land are entrenched, calculated, collaborative, and reactive. The occupiers promise rewards to those who cooperate and dire threats to those who resist. Among the Jewish population of the Land, there is enough animosity to go around—against the occupiers, against the occupiers' Jewish collaborators, between the collaborators and the resistors, and between religious parties who are on opposing ends of the spectrum between rebellion and assimilation. In the next chapter, we will focus on Jewish responses to the opportunities and perceived perils represented and delivered by sea.

The features of this historically conflicting set of assumptions between seafaring expansionists and inland-dwelling defenders are embedded in the story of faith in Scripture. For the seafaring actors in the story, the Mediterranean Sea is indeed the center of their quest for empire building and domination of the people around the sea. For the people of the Land of Israel, the Land, and especially Jerusalem, is the center of the world.[1] These basic conflicting land/sea views underlie directly or indirectly many of the military, cultural, and religious conflicts throughout the entire Scriptures. By the time Paul writes his Epistles, the shorthand for this conflict is "Jew and Greek."

The success of the Roman Empire was inextricably linked to its adaptation to, utilization of, and domination of the Mediterranean Sea. The Greek thalassocracy was now Roman.[2] The defeat of piracy under Pompey in 67 BC is commonly considered to be the decisive, final triumph of Rome's domination of the Mediterranean that created the conditions of control. A closer look at the pirates of the Mediterranean makes the significance of Pompey's victory clearer, for until the threat of piracy was more or less eliminated, the reliability of the system to deliver the needed cargo was always in jeopardy.

Rome had always viewed all Mediterranean pirates as a constant threat. This is understandable. Mediterranean pirates are described by Cicero as "the most bitter, most dangerous adversaries of the Roman people, and what is more, a common foe to peoples and nations everywhere throughout the world."[3] The notorious pirates of Rough Cilicia—the region near which Tarsus is located—were especially

---

1. See Bruce Malina, *The New Testament World: Insights from Cultural Anthropology*, 3rd ed. (Louisville: Westminster John Knox, 2001), 178.

2. The debate about whether the nature of Rome's domination of the Mediterranean constitutes a true thalassocracy is discussed at length in Daniela Maria Dantas Gomes, "Mare Nostrum: Military and Naval Power in Rome (2nd Century BCE–1st Century CE)" (PhD dissertation, University of Lisbon, 2020), http://dx.doi.org/10.13140/RG.2.2.28353.38248. In chapter 4 ("Mare Alterum, Mare Nostrum," 479–544), she provides a thorough discussion of Rome's achievement in dominating the Mediterranean so completely for so long—"Rome's role at sea is not as much in glorious feats in naval battles, but in a warrant of safety and peace of coastal populations, trade and of its own political interests. Its naval power is not born exclusively from the city itself but from its allies and the peoples which it conquers through the centuries. ... Thalassocracy may be a malleable concept ... [but] as a civilisation that uses the sea to control the entirety of a vast empire, Rome being a thalassocracy cannot be argued against" (530).

3. Quoted by Nicholas K. Rauh, *Merchants, Sailors and Pirates in the Roman World* (Stroud, UK: Tempus, 2003), 187.

dangerous.[4] The Cilician pirates, exploiting the rugged, treacherous coastline of Rough Cilicia along a major shipping route between Antioch and Rome, had developed an alternative form of self-government that included a kind of democratic leadership, egalitarian sharing of the spoils, and practice of mutual aid.

Nicholas Rauh's research on the relatively unknown subculture of Mediterranean seafarers gives insightful perspectives on *Mare Nostrum* from the bottom of Roman society during the time of Greek New Testament. Rauh writes, "The so-called Cilician pirates reflected a genuine attempt to challenge social authority on the seas, fomenting not merely rebellion but an underclass programme of reform."[5]

This alternative social organization was eventually viewed by Roman authorities as not only criminal but a genuine maritime rebellion. As is often the case of marginalized groups of outcasts by the established society, "the Cilician pirates constructed their society in defiant opposition to the ways of the world they left behind."[6] Like revolutionary movements in other times and places, they envisioned a world of justice for themselves where their oppressors would be punished. In some ways, they incorporated these ideals into their own counter-society. Rauh describes their social organization:

> In place of the harsh realities of established maritime society, the Cilician pirates appear to have governed themselves

4. Füsun Tülek, "Northeastern Harbors of the Mediterranean Sea on the Cilician Coast and Gulf of Issikos," in *Connecting Cultures: Trade and Interconnections in Ancient Near East from the Beginning until the End of the Roman Period*, ed. Vasıf Şahoğlu, Müge Şevketoğlu, and Yiğit H. Erbil (Ankara: Ankara University Press, 2019), 413–26. This article describes the coastal and riverine harbors and their role and trade in both Rough and Plain Cilicia. Rough Cilician harbors are associated with extensive piracy, whereas Plain Cilician are more legitimate local and long-distance trade connections due to land routes. Rough Cilician harbors were accessible only by sea. Tarsus is on the very western edge of Plain Cilicia, connected by road inland across the Taurus Mountains, and close to the pirate harbors of Rough Cilicia. Pompey evacuated and rebuilt the port towns of Rough Cilicia following the route of pirates in 67 BC. Paul's hometown was on the Cydnus River and was likely linked to the large coastal harbor at Rhegma, especially important as the silting problem of the harbor on the Cydnus River near Tarsus grew. This description of pirates is based on Rauh's excellent research in *Merchants*, 169–201.

5. Rauh, *Merchants*, 191.

6. Rauh, *Merchants*, 191.

> according to a strict code of egalitarianism and social brotherhood. Pirate egalitarianism emerged, at least in part, as a reaction against the hierarchy of the merchant ship and its attendant privileges and abuses.[7]

Thus, in addition to the economic perils of piracy to the Mediterranean shipping, the organized alternative society of the Cilician pirates posed a political threat to Rome.

> Cilician piracy was not simply an economic crime. ... It was a movement in social reform, with thousands of armed seamen organizing themselves into anarchic, yet highly motivated democracies, seeking to provide themselves with more tolerable living conditions, more stable communities, and a fair and more equitable social system."[8]

Rome's ability to combine public sentiment with cruel punishment of Cilician pirates (or Jewish prophets) meant that "if they were captured, they were crucified."[9] A popular public spectacle was the torture and crucifixion of pirates.

But there is another reason to examine the pirates more closely, for while their activity as pirates was sufficiently crushed, those pirates who were not killed, resettled, or enslaved by Pompey's navy continued to live throughout the Mediterranean world. They may have been defeated, but they were not pacified. They would not only find a way to survive within the Roman system, which now needed more sea workers than ever, but they would profit from it. They would find their way aboard ships and into seaports. In the seaports, they would connect with sea workers and travelers from all over the Mediterranean. They would tell stories of Rome's brutality to their children and grandchildren.

---

7. Rauh, *Merchants*, 191.
8. Rauh, *Merchants*, 196.
9. Rauh, *Merchants*, 189.

The descendants of the pirates of the Mediterranean who had been defeated by Pompey continued to nurse resentment. "In the bars and taverns of Mediterranean ports, the anger of the maritime mob [pirates] persisted."[10] There is good reason to believe that descendants of pirates, with residual pirate values, along with many other types of disenfranchised and angry sea workers, found their way to great seaports like Antioch, Corinth, and Ephesus—and very likely into the young seaport churches that Paul founded as well. As with the abused and angry of Jesus' day, the good news attracted the disenfranchised of the sea.

But Pompey had done more than just defeat the Cilician pirates.

> While he was about it he laid the foundation for the revival of the Roman navy and provided the pattern for its organization. The squadrons he had activated were, in the next half-century, to grow into the fleets that fought in Rome's bloody civil wars and, when these had ended, to form the nucleus of the efficient force that turned the Mediterranean into a Roman lake.[11]

The term *Mare Nostrum* then, like *Pax Romana,* includes the brutal repression of any threat of dissent and rebellion anywhere it occurred in the empire. But while the overt activities of those defeated by Rome may have been curtailed, under the surface of compliance the resentments and anger continued to seethe. But not for everyone. Others, connected to the system of control and cooperating with it, could, at least potentially, reap huge rewards. The result was ongoing, simmering social tensions that occasionally exploded. This happened often, in history and the biblical story, in seaports.

In some ways, then, the Mediterranean Sea in the first century can be viewed as being an early form of and functionally equivalent to the internet of the twenty-first century. Globalization today has its historic precedent in the Romanization of the Mediterranean Sea.

---

10. Rauh, *Merchants,* 201.

11. Lionel Casson, *Seafarers and Sea Fighters of the Mediterranean in Ancient Times,* 2nd ed. (Princeton, NJ: Princeton University Press, 1991), 183.

Antisocial screeds, rumors, and conspiracies abounded in the "social media" network of seafarers. The efficient transfer of goods, people, and ideas, especially people and ideas across ethnic and linguistic boundaries, is a feature of both Romanization and globalization. In the first century, fluency in Greek was like fluency in English in our world today: the necessary skill of those who wanted to participate in the exchange of goods and ideas in the connected world of the Mediterranean then or the entire world now.

Andrew Wilson summarizes the significance of Rome's achievements that established the social and historical context of Acts and most of Paul's Epistles:

> The Roman integration of the Mediterranean under a single political system, and the virtual eradication of piracy by Pompey, together with the use of a single currency in nearly all of this area except Egypt, all greatly reduced transaction costs in supplying what had now become a vast pan-Mediterranean market.[12]

The graph below depicts the numbers of shipwrecks dated by century found in the Mediterranean. With Pompey's successful campaign against the pirates of the eastern end of the Mediterranean, shipping surged and reached its height in the first century BC and the first century AD. The high number of shipwrecks in the Mediterranean indicates the level of shipping activity—not the competence of the sailors!

THE INFRASTRUCTURE

There are three components of the infrastructure on which the system of control relied: durable, secure roads; protected sea routes; and seaports in close proximity to functional, all-weather harbors.[13] *Mare*

12. Andrew Wilson, "Developments in Mediterranean Shipping and Maritime Trade from the Hellenistic Period to AD 1000," in *Maritime Archaeology and Ancient Trade in the Mediterranean*, ed. Damian Robinson and Andrew Wilson (Oxford: Oxford Centre for Maritime Archaeology, 2011), 33–60.

13. For a good introduction to Mediterranean shipping, see Andrew Wilson and Damian Robinson, "Introduction: Maritime Archaeology and the Ancient Economy," in Robinson and Wilson, *Maritime Archaeology*, 1–11.

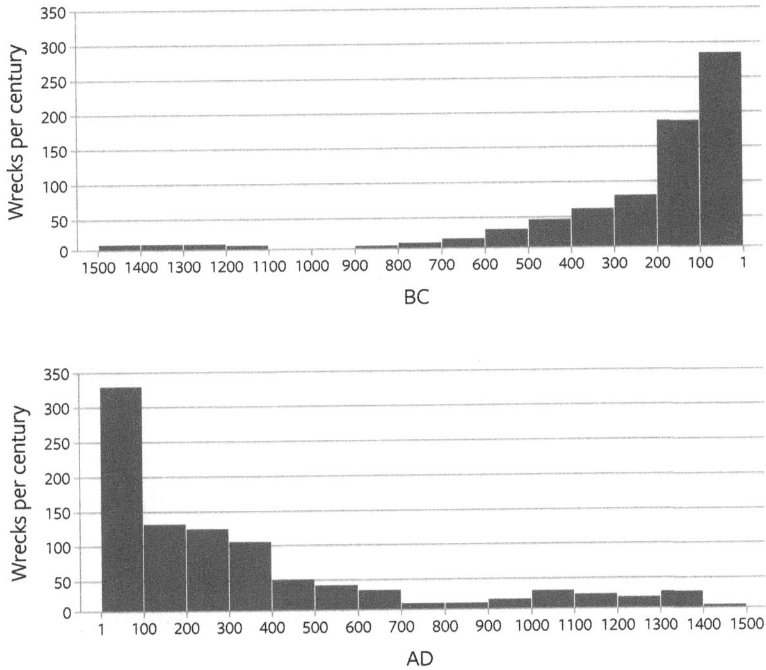

FIGURE 6: **Mediterranean shipwrecks by century, 1500 BC to AD 1500**

Andrew Wilson, "Developments in Mediterranean Shipping and Maritime Trade," in *Maritime Archeology and Ancient Trade in the Mediterranean*, ed. Damian Robinson and Andrew Wilson (Oxford: Oxford Centre for Archeology and Ancient Trade in the Mediterranean, 2011).

Nostrum is only possible when all three of these components of the infrastructure are connected and controlled.

It is estimated that in the Roman period, the Mediterranean was better connected than at any point until the nineteenth century. The connection, control, and coordination of many previously disconnected components of trade in the Mediterranean made the Roman shipping system so successful.[14] The seaports

14. Globalization builds on some of these Roman shipping system innovations. For fascinating modern examples of the development of the coordinated global shipping system that enables wealth by reducing transportation time and costs of goods anywhere in the world, see Marc Levinson, *The Box: How the Shipping Container Made the World Smaller and the World Economy Bigger* (Princeton, NJ: Princeton University Press, 2016), Kindle. For the fascinating and unseen world of cargo ships and their crew, see Rose George, *90 Percent of Everything:*

were the connections, and Rome controlled the connections for its vital interests of expanding and maintaining its power. Control of both land and sea connections for military, political, and economic purposes enabled Rome to dominate the entire population around the Mediterranean and beyond in ways unimaginable at any time before or since. *Mare Nostrum* refers to Rome's ability to establish connections, control them, and protect the spaces between them. To control the Mediterranean was to ensure an uninterrupted supply of wheat from Egypt, salt fish from Judea, and slaves from the conquered territories, as well as the rapid deployment of Rome's brutal peacekeepers. Both the promised rewards for cooperation and the means of brutal punishment for revolt were seaborne. The Mediterranean was the sea of promise or peril for the people connected by the Roman shipping system.

The unprecedented power of the Roman Empire to expand and maintain dominance over the vastly diverse and volatile peoples surrounding the Mediterranean Sea was achieved by its organization and control of human participation on land—roads, legion cities, and military camps—as well as on sea—navy, ports, port cities, and fleets of ships. Sole control of this integrated infrastructure of roads, shipping lanes, islands, and ports gave the Roman Empire the ability to maintain empire-wide trade and dominate the restive population militarily and culturally. This is *Pax Romana*.

Rome's success in the Mediterranean, as with later sea-based empires until modern times, provides the evidence for Adam Smith's observation "that long-distance trade is key to developing wealth and that ships are the most efficient mode of transportation of goods."[15] Rome's military domination of the Mediterranean began a period of peace and stability. Wilson and Robinson describe the "further

---

Inside Shipping, the Invisible Industry That Puts Clothes on Your Back, Gas in Your Car, and Food on Your Plate (New York: Metropolitan Books: 2013).

15. Wilson and Robinson, "Introduction," 1.

institutional developments which completely changed the trading environment":

> The unification of the Mediterranean under Roman rule brought not only peace but also a common set of legal institutions, a single currency ... and further facilitated the spread of the two main lingua franca, Latin and Greek—all of these measures reduced transaction costs. ... [The] entire trading system of the Roman imperial period was possible under the conditions of pan-Mediterranean peace, which removed the variable of warfare-related volatility.[16]

This level of connection had both advantages and disadvantages for the empire. On the one hand, the wealthy and privileged of the Roman elite class could enjoy the natural resources and productivity of regions originating far away from Rome. These distant regions, with their abundant supplies of exotic food, slaves, and luxury goods of every kind, flowed continually toward Rome and the wealthy cities of the empire.

Military and cultural power also flowed toward the distant regions. Powerful, attractive, and creative Greek philosophical and scientific ideas were spread throughout the empire by the constant movement on sea and land by the workers who carried the goods. Roman officials carried the propaganda of the rulers. Traders carried goods. Soldiers carried weapons.

There were disadvantages for the elite to be connected to the people they exploited. The marginalized and exploited, the enslaved and abused, the poor and the desperate were as connected as the wealthy elite. Slaves carried resentment. The sea workers carried dangerous news of resistance from places like Judea and Alexandria. The manual laborers trying to survive financially carried their desperation and resentment from place to place. The increasing disparity was connected by land and sea and guaranteed that the ever-present

16. Wilson and Robinson, "Introduction," 7, 9.

simmering resistance of the dissatisfied and desperate would inevitably explode into violent uprisings as well as popular alternative social movements that threatened Rome's control of the hearts and minds of the population. The incitement to violence and the influence of attractive alternative social ideas could be transported on the Roman system as easily as the threats and promises of the empire.

This is the world of the New Testament, especially the story from Acts to Revelation. The Christian movement benefited from the Roman system of connections. Its attractive ideas were carried by the dissatisfied and disillusioned and resonated with not only their peers on and around the Mediterranean but also the powerful elite of the urban centers.

How does Rome, or any empire, maintain control of the sea indefinitely? Rome's most effective control of the sea for four hundred years was the control of the activity of the diverse peoples who lived around the rim of the sea and sailed the routes between ports. Rome dominated the Mediterranean by controlling the connections, the ports of the Mediterranean, and the cities connected directly to them. It controlled and utilized the islands of the Mediterranean to protect the shipping lanes and the seaports and to isolate rebels. Rome controlled any place where either friends or foes could launch a boat of any significant size with the intent to profit from the domination of Rome—or to challenge it. To control humans energized by hope and connected to those desperate for change would become, in time, almost impossible for Rome. In the meantime, the Roman navy would be key.

Control of the restive populations of seaports and resentful seafarers requires the continuous presence of a massive navy. Rome had the resources and ability to organize huge building projects. It had procured, as the empire expanded across the northern shores of the Mediterranean, access to the vast forests necessary for building its huge fleet of ships, and it began felling these mighty forests that grew on the mountain riverbanks. This deforestation eventually was so extensive that those mountain rivers began to wash the loosened soil into the very river-mouth harbors that the navy was created to protect, gradually rendering them useless. The Roman navy might control the people on and around the Mediterranean, but it could not control, or even foresee, the long-term effects of its ecological destruction in the Mediterranean basin.[17]

Rome's navy patrolled the shipping lanes. The legionaries and auxiliaries built, maintained, and patrolled the fifty thousand miles (80,000 km) of roads around the entire rim of the Mediterranean that were eventually completed, an accomplishment only Rome ever achieved.[18] By building an infrastructure of connections and a system of protecting this infrastructure on land and sea, Rome achieved its greatest success. And it was on this success that the good news of the kingdom of God was carried.

The role of the inhabited and connected islands of the Mediterranean in Rome's control of the shipping lanes and population is critical. The combination of insularity and connectivity makes islands distinct from mainland seaports—"centrality of the islands in the moving of goods, merchandise, traders, travellers, and soldiers in the Late Antique Mediterranean is confirmed by nautical texts."[19]

The islands of the Mediterranean, especially the islands of the Aegean along the sea routes through which a large percentage of shipping occurred, were among the most important strategically for the Roman navy to control. The great cities on the shores of the Aegean needed protection as well. The picturesque islands of the Aegean, fortified by Rome, formed a buffer between the sea and the mainland. And because the only access to the islands from the mainland was by ship, which Rome monitored and controlled, islands made ideal places to isolate troublemakers of all kinds. Augustus exiled his own daughter, for instance, when her scandalous escapades had become

17. While scientific data allows modern empires to foresee the consequences of ecological destruction and enables the potential to slow human contributions to it, the economic and political costs make any significant change extremely difficult.

18. This estimate by historians of fifty thousand miles (80,000 km) of paved road in the Roman Empire is based on the so-called Peutinger Map. This medieval map is a copy of a Roman road map that depicts the road system that encircled the entire Mediterranean Sea.

19. Salvatore Cosentino, "Mentality, Technology and Commerce: Shipping amongst the Mediterranean Islands in Late Antiquity and Beyond," in *The Insular System of the Early Byzantine Mediterranean*, ed. Demetrios Michaelides, Philippe Pergola, and Enrico Zanini, British Archaeological Reports International Series 2523 (Oxford: Archaeopress, 2013), 65–76.

an embarrassment. But it was people of influence, especially those accused of sedition or conspiracy, such as John, leader of the church in Ephesus, whom Rome needed to control. Troublemakers could easily be silenced by isolation on an island. There are only two islands mentioned by name in the Hebrew Scripture. In contrast, there are twelve mentioned in the Greek New Testament, eleven in Acts and one in Revelation. Those mentioned in Acts demonstrate the shipping network, while Patmos, a small island just off the main coastal shipping route, was part of the security system of the Roman navy.

TABLE 1: **The islands of Scripture**

Hebrew Scripture	
Arvad	Ezek 27:8, 11
Kittim (Cyprus)	Gen 10:4; Num 24:24; 1 Chr 1:7; Dan 11:30
Cyprus	Isa 23:1, 12; Jer 2:10; Ezek 27:6
Greek Apocrypha	
Kittim (Cyprus)	1 Macc 1:1
Cyprus	1 Macc 15:23; 2 Macc 10:13; 12:2
Crete	1 Macc 10:67
Rhodes	1 Macc 15:23
Samos	1 Macc 15:23
Greek New Testament	
Cauda	Acts 27:16
Chios	Acts 20:15
Cos	Acts 21:1
Crete	Acts 27:7, 12–14, 21; Titus 1:5
Cyprus	Acts 4:36; 11:19, 20; 13:4; 15:39; 21:3, 16; 27:4
Malta	Acts 28:1
Mitylene	Acts 20:14
Patmos	Rev 1:9
Rhodes	Acts 21:1
Samos	Acts 20:15

The larger islands along the route described in Acts of the apostle Paul on his final return to Judea at the end of his third journey back to Jerusalem identify the exact route with sailing times (Acts 20:14–21:3). This shipping route includes mainland ports: Assos, Mitylene, Chios, Samos, Miletus, Cos, Rhodes, and Patara, ending in Tyre. All the ports between Assos at the beginning of the voyage and Tyre at the end are islands except Miletus and Patara, both in present-day Turkey and key trading seaports at the time. All of the islands on this busy route are either key trading partners, key navy bases, or both. Patmos, the small, inhabited island where John was banished, just outside of the shipping lanes, was primarily used for security purposes by the Romans.

Ships

From the Phoenicians, Rome learned to build excellent ships. The strong hull construction and effective, flexible sailing rigs meant that Roman ships could sail the whole length of the Mediterranean if required. Ships could sail straight from one major port to another, or they might go from port to port along the coast, picking up new cargo and unloading old cargoes as they went. As the shipping system developed, the Mediterranean Sea functioned as a major hub of travel and communication. The seaports were connected to inland trade routes, and with routes connecting to the Red Sea, the known world became a network of trade, centered on the Mediterranean.[20]

Most of the ships in the Mediterranean were built using mortise-and-tenon construction. The builders constructed the outer planking of the vessel first, each plank joined to the one above with hundreds of mortise-and-tenon joints and locked in place with small pegs. A framework was then added to the inside of the vessel to provide additional reinforcement. Although it was time consuming to build ships and boats

20. "King Solomon built a fleet of ships at Ezion-geber, which is near Eloth on the shore of the Red Sea, in the land of Edom. Hiram sent his servants with the fleet, sailors who were familiar with the sea, together with servants of Solomon. They went to Ophir, and imported from there ... gold" (1 Kgs 9:26–28). See 2 Chronicles 8:17–18 for the parallel passage. *The Periplus of the Eythraean Sea* by an unknown first-century author is an often-cited description of the shipping that connected the Mediterranean to Africa and India.

in this way, it resulted in very strong, durable vessels, and this construction method was used in the Mediterranean for many centuries.

From the dawn of ancient shipping in the Mediterranean and into the Roman era, a distinguishing accomplishment of *Mare Nostrum* was the establishment of long-distance, scheduled shipping. Casson writes, "Probably the most ambitious maritime enterprise of the ancient world was the transport of the tribute in grain that Rome levied on Egypt, 150,000 tons which traveled annually from Alexandria to Rome during the first three centuries A.D. and required the services of a fleet of the biggest and fastest freighters available."[21]

Long-distance ships were the supertankers of Rome. Grain for animal and human consumption was the fuel of the Roman Empire. With its huge population, Rome was a net importer of fuel for the entire population, including the cadres of workers who toiled in the endless construction projects. Large quantities of grain were an absolute necessity. Riots could occur during food shortages. Food security helped keep the population pacified. Additionally, access to reliable sources of grain to feed the far-flung armies constantly fighting and building across the empire required a fleet of such supertankers and the coordination of a long-distance shipping system, especially from the fertile Egyptian delta. These ships were specially designed for the route between Alexandria and Rome. One round trip per year was common, and under the right weather conditions and if a ship's owner and captain were willing to take some risks, a second, highly profitable round trip might be attempted. This is the story in Acts 27, which incidentally is one of the rare eyewitness accounts of a first-century shipwreck, and only one of two reliable texts that offer much information about the grain ships of Rome.[22]

---

21. Lionel Casson, *Ships and Seamanship in the Ancient World* (Baltimore, MD: The Johns Hopkins University Press, 1995), 297. Casson describes the one to two round-trips per year that the grain fleet could make between Rome and Alexandria, the routes, and the challenges required to feed Rome (297–99).

22. See Nicolle Hirschfeld, "The Ship of Saint Paul: Historical Background," *Biblical Archaeologist* 53 (1990): 25–30, for summary details of Roman grain ships.

Roman ships built in the mortise-and-tenon tradition could reach huge sizes. The largest excavated cargo ship comes from the site of Madrague de Giens in the South of France. It was over forty meters in length and could have carried a cargo of around four hundred tons. On its last voyage in the first century BC, it had seven to ten thousand Italian wine amphorae on board, destined for southern Gaul. Some of the largest ships of the Roman period were likely grain ships—estimated between one thousand and twelve hundred metric tons.[23]

The coastal freighter, the average Roman ship, was far smaller, perhaps around fifteen to twenty meters, and capable of carrying seventy-five tons of cargo. According to Wilson, "the majority of merchant, cargo ships were under 100 tons."[24] There is enough evidence from shipwrecks and their cargoes, as well as the archaeological remains of small harbor installations around the rim of the Mediterranean, to conclude that most goods circulated on a small scale, within local networks, and that the majority of ships were rather small, coastal freighters. These would work their way up and down "along known coastlines and between socially connected communities. ... A distinctly regional scale of seaborne connectivity played a fundamental role in structuring maritime interaction and market formation."[25]

Although the method of construction was similar across the Roman Mediterranean, the shapes of the hulls were not. Some vessels were quite flat-bottomed so that they could work in shallow water and up and down rivers, canals, and estuaries. Meanwhile, other vessels had very deep keels shaped like a wine glass that allowed them to sail more effectively. Many vessels carried a bird's head on the stern of the vessel, and some ships had an underwater projection at the bow, like the bow of a modern tanker, to cut through the water more efficiently. All of the ships of the Roman Mediterranean were

23. Wilson, "Developments," 40.

24. Wilson, "Developments," 39.

25. Wilson, "Developments," 32–33.

FIGURE 7: **Relief of a ship with a steering oar in the ancient site of Corinth**

powered by rowing or sailing, as can be seen from many mosaics and carved reliefs.

Remains of the sails themselves are very rare in the archaeological record, and most of the known finds come from the Roman ports on the Egyptian Red Sea coast. But the mosaics and reliefs show us that the majority of vessels were rigged with a square sail, usually a single large sail, or sometimes two square sails on two masts. Some smaller vessels, such as the tugboats and harbor boats found at Portus, used a different type of sail called a spritsail, which was better for working in the more confined spaces of the harbor basins.

The rigging used on the Mediterranean square sail is unique to this period in history. It consisted of many small rings, made from wood, lead, or horn, that were sewn onto the face of the sail. These rings, called brail rings, guided a series of lines that could be hauled on from the deck to change the shape of the sail, reduce its size in stronger wind, and furl it when needed. Unlike on vessels in later periods, no crew needed to climb the rigging to trim or take in the sails.

Sailing ships in the Roman period did not need large crews. The square sail that was used by the majority of vessels was efficient, and archaeological remains, along with experimental voyaging using replicas of Roman ships, tell us that a crew of four or five people could operate a single-mast ship of about one hundred fifty tons. Sailing vessels were therefore the most favored for carrying cargo because they were much cheaper to operate. Warships were usually powered by oars, which meant that they were not reliant on the wind. But their large crews were expensive to maintain, and their need for food and water meant that their range of warships was limited.

The Mediterranean square sail allowed the grain ships to sail at a steady speed day and night. In good weather, with a favorable wind from the side or behind, a vessel could reach average speeds of between four and six knots. If the wind was blowing in the wrong direction, progress was very slow, and only the most well-maintained vessels with the best crews were able to sail against the wind at an angle of no more than sixty or seventy degrees. Literary sources suggest that most sailors preferred to wait in port for better weather.

In the ancient world, navigation was based on careful observation of the environment: the sun, stars, and weather conditions. By doing this, and drawing upon many centuries of learned knowledge, sailors could navigate their way comfortably around the Mediterranean. They could sail on courses that took them out of sight of land, and they were able to sail through the night, finding their way by the stars. The most common piece of equipment was a lead sounding weight. This not only allowed the depth of the water to be established but also recovered a sample of the seabed, and an experienced navigator could use this extra information to help maintain a course or sense when land was approaching but still out of sight.

The key to the success of the vast and incessant exchange of goods in the Roman era in the Mediterranean is the web of connections between producers and consumers, between local and long-distance transportation links. With the social networking possible within *Pax Romana* that included trade laws, predictable markets, secure trade routes, and a common trade language, the conditions for the explosion of Mediterranean trade were in place. Business boomed. Looking back, "there is a growing awareness of the role played by webs of personal and community relationships in structuring exchange systems."[26]

Shipping along coastal routes from port to port, known as cabotage, includes independent ship operators picking up available cargo and delivering it to its destination within a limited region. While most attention is focused on the large vessels and long-distance routes of the Roman shipping system, cabotage and coastal shipping comprised the majority of shipping activity in the Mediterranean. While both coastal shipping and cabotage are relatively short-distance operations, coastal shipping likely included fixed routes, whereas cabotage was opportunistic—that is, picking up any available cargo destined for delivery to a destination that was profitable. This made shipping—and coastal travel by sea for passengers—less predictable than ships sailing on fixed routes, both short and long distances, as the story in Acts demonstrates. This distinction may shed light, for instance, on Paul's choice to walk from Troas to Assos (Acts 20:5–6, 13). The ship planned to sail to Assos but may have taken on some last-minute available cargo to be delivered to a destination that clearly delayed its expected arrival. Paul could save time by walking but, having paid for the journey in advance, wanted his traveling companions to remain aboard to ensure that he could rejoin the ship in Assos and continue the journey for which they had all paid. While this is speculative, unnamed shipping variables typical of cabotage are almost certainly behind the route and schedule of the coastal voyage between Troas and Tyre described in Acts 20–21.[27]

26. Justin Leidwanger, "Maritime Networks and Economic Regionalism in the Roman Eastern Mediterranean," *Les Nouvelles de l'archéologie* 135 (2014): 32.

27. There is good evidence that most goods circulated on a small scale, within local networks. The evidence for this assertion is based on tracing of pottery fragments that demonstrate

Harbors

The harbors of the Mediterranean are ancient. John Oleson describes the conditions that raised the need for the harbors:

> The Mediterranean Sea provided nearly ideal conditions for seafaring in antiquity, and the many islands drew mariners out on boats from a very early period. ... Travel by ship became essential to the survival of the many cultures around the shores of the sea. As ships became larger, and the demands of trade more complex harbours were needed to shelter ships and to provide easy access for people and goods.[28]

As Ezekiel 27 depicts, other seafaring peoples had traded extensively long before the Romans. The Egyptians, Phoenicians, Greeks, and others generally began with naturally sheltered rivers, beaches, and bays. Over time, these natural harbors would be improved to accommodate larger ships and increase protection from the elements or enemies, the latter being accomplished by building a breakwater with a small opening across which a chain could be suspended.

Oleson notes, "there was no real further progress in harbour engineering until the development of hydraulic concrete by the Romans around 200 B.C."[29] The discovery of the formula for concrete that would harden under water allowed not only the improvement of natural harbors but the construction of completely artificial harbors, such as in Caesarea in Judea, the first and one of the largest completely artificial harbors in the Mediterranean at that time.[30]

---

distribution patterns and on the proximity and products of very small ports that made short-distance shipping both possible and necessary. For an excellent article that demonstrates the role of small seaports connected to large shipping centers, see Robert L. Hohlfelder and Robert L. Vann, "Cabotage at Aperlae in Ancient Lycia," *International Journal of Nautical Archaeology* 29 (2000): 126–35.

28. John Peter Oleson, "The Evolution of Harbour Engineering in the Ancient Mediterranean World," in *Harbors and Harbor Cities in the Eastern Mediterranean from Antiquity to the Byzantine Period: Recent Discoveries and Current Approaches*, ed. Sabine Ladstaetter, Felix Pirson, and Thomas Schmidts (Istanbul: Ege Yayinlari, 2014), 509.

29. Oleson, "The Evolution," 515.

30. For a more complete description of this and other artificial Roman harbors, see Oleson, "The Evolution," 516.

Many key ports and thriving port cities are mentioned in Acts. Two of the primary ports between Rome and the Aegean are Ephesus and Corinth, the two cities where Paul spends the greatest amount of time and where highly influential churches are planted. The wealth and power of these and other ports depend on two key factors: a good natural harbor facility and a location that generates a high level of traffic as a hub, linking land and sea routes. Katia Schörle notes the significance of the location: "The traffic factor is the most important one; excellent natural harbour sites will not be used unless of economic value for the area ... and harbours will be constructed artificially if needed, according to the technology available."[31]

Rome could develop and defend a system of the entire Mediterranean into which the technological advances and feats of engineering were integrated, making *Mare Nostrum* a reality. Wilson observes, "Technological factors enabled, but did not drive the process; more important in this regard were institutional developments. Laws of contract, maritime loans, and sea laws existed ... and provided a necessary framework for large-scale maritime trade."[32]

These human resources were the maritime skills and seamanship of Roman sailors and navigators, the administrative genius of Rome, and the military capacity to control the entire Mediterranean Sea. Rome's connections and its control of these connections resulted in the domination of the people of the seaports and ships. This domination yielded some basic benefits for the dominated people who cooperated with the empire. But its benefits were especially for the dominators.

Seafarers

Insight into the story of the Gospels, Acts, Paul's Epistles, and the early Christian communities around the Mediterranean rim is enriched

---

31. Katia Schörle, "Constructing Port Hierarchies: Harbours of the Central Tyrrhenian Coast," in Robinson and Wilson, *Maritime Archaeology*, 93.

32. Wilson, "Developments," 54.

by an awareness of the culture of the sea workers in the first century. Jesus and Paul relied on sea workers for their ministry. It was sea workers both aboard boats and ships and in the ports of their respective seas with whom they spent so much time.

Sea workers, whether on the Sea of Galilee or on the Mediterranean Sea, were seen as low status by the rest of society. If the sea workers were Jewish, such as fishermen on the Sea of Galilee, they were usually ritually unclean and held in some disdain, especially by the urban Jews of Jerusalem. If the sea workers were in the Mediterranean, they were pagan, not only unclean from the Jewish point of view but living examples of depravity and evil. They were to be avoided. All were generally poor. For these reasons, religious Jews in the first century sought to avoid travel by ship unless absolutely necessary.[33] Both Jesus and Paul move from tolerating seafaring to embracing it as a preferred mode of transportation and even to identifying with low-status seafarers. This has strategic, ecclesiological, and theological implications in both Jesus' and Paul's missions.

Sea workers were the necessary evil of the Roman economy connected by the Mediterranean Sea for the first and last time in history. The vaunted Roman shipping system was built on the blood, sweat, and often-early deaths of the sea workers.

At the top of the seafaring social status pyramid were the merchants, traders, ship owners, and captains of large ships. It was these maritime opportunists, the risk takers, who assembled the trade routes in the highly unstable conditions of maritime trade. "Unlike land-holding elements, ancient merchants willfully exposed themselves to an inescapable variety of dangers," explains Rauh.[34] Even compared to small farmers, seafarers are associated with an inferior occupation. Libanius' (AD 314–93) comparison of seafaring to farming seems to capture the sentiment of the intellectual elite toward

33. In the next chapter we will further examine why Jewish travel by sea in the New Testament was avoided if there were other good options.

34. Rauh, *Merchants*, 139.

seafaring embedded in Roman culture from its early domination of the Mediterranean. According to Cosentino, Libanius

> compared navigation with agriculture. ... He argued the superiority of the latter over the former in five arguments, which we may summarize as follows: 1) whereas agriculture is natural, navigation has been conceived by humans for making profit; 2) land is safe, whereas the sea is dangerous; 3) countryside is sweet, sea is dreadful; 4) the countryside is healthy, the sea is unhealthy; 5) wealth coming from the land is long-lasting, while that coming from maritime commerce is ephemeral.[35]

Although these seafarers of *Mare Nostrum* were disdained by the elites of the empire, they could become extremely wealthy. While often emerging from lower social strata from the rougher eastern end of the Mediterranean, they were keen businessmen with the knowledge and skills necessary to run a successful enterprise.[36]

> These were the "big shots" of the everyday maritime world, the kind of men ordinary traders, shippers, sailors and slaves looked up to and aspired to become. ... The maritime world was both coarse and violent; it was definitely no place for the weak. ... Roman traders assessed the risks of a maritime venture and gambled with both their lives and their livelihoods.[37]

Fabulous wealth could be made, but wealth alone only went so far in gaining social status. "Almost universally the sources decry their behavior as rapacious, corrupt, ruthless and sometimes downright murderous."[38]

But still, this class of business entrepreneurs was far above the laboring class of seamen who did the manual labor. Although all

35. Cosentino, "Mentality," 65.
36. Rauh, *Merchants*, 139.
37. Rauh, *Merchants*, 141.
38. Rauh, *Merchants*, 145.

maritime workers were risk takers, those at the top were ready to risk losing their investments. Those at the bottom risked losing their lives, not only from the dangerous sea and shoreline of the Mediterranean but from those in authority. Describing their precarious existence, Rauh writes, "The common seaman ... could be dispatched into harm's way under any circumstances. In a word, Roman merchants essentially controlled the course of maritime life for all who labored beneath them; a common sailor could only pursue the fate his wages assigned."[39]

Passengers in the Roman Mediterranean, including Paul and the early Christians, were thrust together with sea workers for extended periods of time. Who were these sea workers? Who would choose the hard, marginalized, and dangerous life of a sea worker, and why? The primary motivation seems to be survival. The meager wages and slavery of the labor system of Rome "drove ancient seamen away from official society as they had known it, and towards fundamentally different ways of life on the margins of the sea."[40] Rauh states that the "ancient sailors were the cast-offs of the Mediterranean society, freeborn as often as they were slave. ... While more fortunate workers found employment as agricultural day labourers, artisans, and dockyard stevedores, the truly destitute, used-up and socially discarded elements were pushed out onto the sea."[41] The common sailors, at the bottom of the social world of seafaring, were people whom Rauh calls the "maritime mob."[42]

The résumés of seafarers in the first century included former pirates from Cilicia, Pamphylia, and Lycia; runaway slaves; unemployed soldiers; and criminals running from the authorities, as well as

---

39. Rauh, *Merchants*, 145.

40. Rauh, *Merchants*, 132.

41. Rauh, *Merchants*, 161.

42. Nicholas K. Rauh et al., "*Ochlos Nautikos:* Leisure Culture and Underclass Discontent in the Roman Maritime World," in *The Maritime World of Ancient Rome: Proceedings of "The Maritime World of Ancient Rome" Conference Held at the American Academy in Rome 27–29 March 2003*, ed. Robert L. Hohlfelder (Ann Arbor, MI: University of Michigan Press, 2008), 197–242. The author uses the term "maritime mob" to describe the similarity of Mediterranean pirates' organization and methods to those observable in modern "mobs."

those who provided services to the seafarers, such as prostitutes and pimps.[43] For all of these marginalized, low-status, and poor workers, the sea offered the ability to survive and escape abuse, prosecution, slavery, and death. They could disappear on the margins of the society that the sea provided. But these sea workers "remained essential cogs to the system of primitive accumulation" by providing the necessary knowledge and labor that powered merchant shipping.[44]

As a group, they were both connected and mobile and formed a kind of alternative society distinct from the land dwellers who looked at them with distaste and suspicion—"sailors and sea-traders were regarded as foreigners. The men of the maritime community were outsiders—misfits, adventurers, entrepreneurs, and anyone else who chose the sea as a way of life."[45] The social dynamics of the seaports and their early church communities are the context of Acts and Paul's struggle to establish his authority in ports, especially Corinth. So while the sea workers were the "necessary evil" of the empire, they were the "necessary good" of the kingdom.

According to Marcus Rediker, "seamen were in many ways nomads, voyaging without firm geographical boundaries or stable residence, and their mobility insured a rapid diffusion of their culture."[46] Like fishermen on the Sea of Galilee, connected nomads were disseminators of news. "The mobile seaman was both a carrier of information and ideas between different groups of laboring people and someone

43. See Rauh, *Merchants*, 162–67, for additional description of sea workers.

44. Rauh, *Merchants*, 187.

45. Janet Wade, "Sailors, Merchants and the Maritime Cults that Sailed into the Ports (and Streets) of Early Byzantium," in *Byzantium, Its Neighbours and Its Cultures*, Byzantina Australiensia 20, ed. Danijel Dzino and Ken Parry (Leiden: Brill, 2014), 281. Although Wade's study is from late antiquity, it is descriptive of the ongoing, entrenched characteristics of sea-worker culture that originate in antiquity and continue to persist in the Christian era.

46. Marcus Rediker, *Between the Devil and the Deep Blue Sea* (Cambridge: Cambridge University Press, 1987), 158. While Rediker's study is of eighteenth-century merchant seamen and pirates of the Anglo-American maritime world, it is considered by Rauh and others to be descriptive of the social dynamics of maritime workers in general throughout history, particularly that of the vast Roman shipping empire on the Mediterranean in the first century.

who by way of new experiences was sometimes able to generate new ideas and practices."[47]

The sea-worker fraternity formed a self-reliant, self-organized alternative to the social structure of the Roman Empire. The alternative maritime culture of the sea workers emerged from and was nurtured by a shared experience of abuse and exploitation at the hands of higher-class Romans.

The sea workers treated their enemies, especially Roman authorities, harshly; mocked conventions; and often flouted decorum and morality. Their antiauthoritarian subculture clashed with those in authority, whether they were representatives of Roman rule or the commanders of the ship. Thus, as Anastasia Godolou concludes, "the sea both divides and unites people."[48] The ships on which Paul spent so much time were divided, with those on the bottom united against those on the top and vice versa.[49]

Leaders of the sea workers at the bottom did not inherit or buy their respect and influence—they earned it.

> Among the experiences and characteristics that earned a seaman authority and esteem were an understanding of the techniques and technicalities of the work place, knowledge of the trade routes and the sea's winding geography, a command of maritime vocabulary, having survived a shipwreck or two, a good singing voice or a nimble dancing step, physical strength and courage, good humour, and among the men at the bottom of the labouring, scars on one's back from the whips of social superiors—telltale symbols of defiance and endurance.[50]

---

47. Rediker, *Between*, 163.

48. Anastasia Gadolou, "Life on Board," in *The Antikythera Shipwreck: The Ship, the Treasures, the Mechanism*, ed. Nikolaos Kaltsas, Elena Vlachogianni, and Polyxeni Bouyia (Athens: Hellenic Ministry of Culture and Tourism, National Archaeological Museum, 2012), 51.

49. An excellent example of division aboard a first-century grain ship is in the account of the sailors attempting to abandon the ship along with the captain, soldiers, and passengers on the shipwreck on Malta. According to Luke's account in Acts 27, Paul seems to be the only person aboard who can keep everyone cooperating long enough for all to survive.

50. Rauh, *Merchants*, 163.

Further descriptions of seafarers include the defiance of physical abuse, the ability to endure pain, and the ability to even laugh and boast about it.[51]

Seafarers were instrumental in spreading the Christian movement in the Mediterranean and, more importantly, in shaping the character of the Christian communities of the seaports. Their constant movement at sea and their presence in the main seaports are part of the Acts story to which we will turn in chapter 5. Paul's establishment of authority in the seaport churches and his teaching to those churches in which seafarers almost certainly participated seem to be related to the values and behavior of the seafaring underclass that included former pirates.

> Pirate crews elected their captains and expected them to act as bold leaders in combat and fair administrators of justice. Crews organized themselves through written articles of agreement and cemented the loyalty of all new members by swearing them to the most dreadful sacred oaths. By these means, they were able to form counter-cultural communities socially isolated from mainstream Mediterranean hierarchies. ... Pirates sustained their communities generationally, supporting women, children and disabled pirates in a manner wholly inconceivable during their previous existence as seamen.[52]

In the major seaports such as Corinth and Ephesus, and inevitably in the Christian community, the presence of seafarers created tension

---

51. The cultural similarities between sea workers in the first century and in the twentieth century (prior to the revolution that containerization created) are remarkable. "Harsh working conditions, economic uncertainty, and the insularity of docker life gave rise to unique mores. Dockworkers saw themselves as tough, independent men doing a very tough job. William Pilcher, studying longshoremen while working as one, found that his colleagues cherished and cultivated reputations as drinkers and brawlers. 'They like to see themselves as rough-and-ready individuals, and that is the image they present to outsiders and to one another,' Pilcher observed. That self-image was also the public's image. A British survey published in 1950 placed dockers twenty-ninth among thirty professions in status, above only road sweepers, at a time when dockers earned more than the average national wage. That judgment was the same among both men and women and among people of all social classes." Levinson, *The Box*, 34.

52. Rauh, *Merchants*, 195.

partly because they were seen as untrustworthy and partly because of their reputation for immorality. Marginalized men with few options were attracted to seafaring because of the appeal and promise of completely unrestrained freedom, including unlimited drinking, easy sexual access to women, and other vices that Paul describes, writing from Corinth, as shameful and debased (Rom 1).

SAMARIA AND BEYOND

The book of Acts moves quickly into a sweeping story of movement, confrontations, explanations, and people with non-Jewish names playing key roles. It is the people mentioned in the early chapters of Acts and the places from which they came that are intriguing. "There was a Levite, a native of Cyprus" (Acts 4:36). Cyprus was a famously powerful, wealthy, and thoroughly pagan island and a famous center of Aphrodite worship. The apostles call this man Barnabas.

The seven deacons chosen to help with the distribution of food among the Hellenized Jewish widows in Jerusalem are themselves, as their names indicate, Hellenized Jews. One is even a gentile convert to Judaism who comes from Antioch, a major seaport rivaling Rome and Alexandria (Acts 6:1–6).[53] Another of the newly selected deacons, Stephen, quickly engages other Hellenized Jews in debate and ends up at a hearing before the Sanhedrin for his efforts. His speech, in which he makes the case for the relative unimportance of the Land of Israel and the temple in Jerusalem, earns him the death penalty (Acts

53. The appointment of these Hellenized Jews likely contributes to the importance of sea connections to how Jesus' mandate to the "ends of the earth" would be fulfilled. As Hellenized Jews, some of whom are residents of seaports and who had likely arrived in Palestine by ship, their presence and then leadership in the growing faith community in Jerusalem almost certainly exert an early influence in the community in Jerusalem toward the sea, seaports, and the people who lived in them. Stephen's initial appearance before the "synagogue of the Freedmen" (Acts 6:9) included Hellenized Jews from seaports: Cyrene, Alexandria, and the southern coast of Asia. By the time of the story of Peter's seaside vision in Joppa, the movement of the apostles in the direction of the coastal area and the interaction of Hellenized Jewish believers relating with Hellenized observant Jews have already begun to change the perception toward the sea and its people, as well as the potential of "the ends of the earth" for the good news of the kingdom.

6:8–7:60). This is witnessed by many Jews in Jerusalem, including the young Saul from the seaport of Tarsus (Acts 7:58).

The shift resulting from the "push" of persecution, and the "pull" of the Spirit's direction, is relentlessly toward the Mediterranean Sea. Philip, another of the selected deacons, preaches in Samaria, then is directed to go down toward Gaza, the old Philistine city on the shore of the Mediterranean (Acts 8:26). After his encounter with the Ethiopian courtier on his way back home, Philip ends up in Samaria.

THE CULTURAL HEGEMONY

The Mediterranean Sea was the liquid, pagan center of the Roman Empire. It was the domination and utilization of this sea that enabled Rome to subdue the variety of powerful ethnic groups around the entire rim of the Mediterranean, to consolidate their vast resources, and to redirect the longings of these individuals and groups toward the enhancement of Rome's self-interest. This was a remarkable achievement. Rome demonstrated that by utilizing the sea and eliminating anyone else who tried to do the same, its control of the people and resources around the Mediterranean could grow without limit. Sea-based empires ever since Rome have sought to emulate this vision of limitless expansion on vastly larger seas. The effort by world empires to control the seas continues to this day.

The political power and economic promises of Rome rode the waves of the sea not only to seaports like Tarsus but all the way to Jerusalem in Judea, which was now a part of the Roman Empire. For the inhabitants of the Land of Israel, the power and glory of Israel's past kings and God's promises were faded memories of the past or remote, far-fetched dreams of the future. Rome ruled in the present, and by all indications, the future belonged to Rome as well.

While the relative safety of sea travel provided possibilities for the wealthy and curious of the Roman Empire to marvel at the renowned human achievements on display around the Mediterranean, every major harbor around the Mediterranean was also a showcase of the power and success of the pagan empire of Rome. Temples to the gods and emperors, even in Caesarea in Judea, dominated the high ground above many harbors, while others boasted spectacular temples literally at the water's edge. Monuments commemorating the achievements of the emperors as well as shopping areas and theaters immediately adjacent to the harbors were common.

The promises of personal power and glory, potentially available for all who believe the compelling evidence that surrounds them and who strive to attain the rewards achieved by others within the system, are powerful. Roman promises were both repugnant and attractive to the Jews of Judea, dividing the community. As Judea was integrated into the Roman system of cultural influence, Jewish society increasingly reflected and reacted to the threat and promises of this influence.

By the beginning of the first century AD, the triumph of Rome must have seemed complete. The empire's expansion to the rest of the world seemed inevitable, even to many Jews living in the stubborn Roman province of Judea. But as the power and promise of the empire were on the rise, "in the days of Caesar Augustus" (Luke 2:1) Jesus was born. The power and promise of another kingdom, the kingdom of God, would connect and compete with the empire of Rome.

REFLECTIONS FROM THE SEA

I was sailing "single-handed." It was four o'clock in the morning and, except for the spectacular stars in the heavens, pitch dark. It was to be a long day, sailing south along the Turkish coast from the ancient harbor of the Lycian city, Phaselis, in the Gulf of Antalya, past Finike, our home port, then twenty miles (32 km) farther to the safe harbor of Kekova. So an early start was necessary to make it in the daylight. The forecast had predicted the wind direction to be near-perfect, directly behind me the entire way, a very rare occurrence. In the protected waters of the anchorage, I had set the sails, wing-on-wing, with the headsail poled out to catch the following wind. The wind and waves were rising by the time I finished the demanding job alone.

I had just settled into the cockpit when I noticed, several miles away, a string of lights. It appeared to be a convoy of some kind, navy I presumed. It was many miles away, many miles long. I could not see the end of it. Whose navy? I wondered.

I flew along in the darkness, enjoying the growing light on the eastern horizon, at peace with the world, until I noticed a Turkish Coast Guard vessel approaching at high speed. I watched warily, still flying along. When it was about fifty yards away, it slowed suddenly, then matched my speed. I could see a crew member on deck with a bullhorn through which, a minute later, he hailed me in English: "You must turn back."

"Why?" I shouted.

"Navy convoy," he bull-horned back. "Must stay away."

"Whose navy?"

"USA."

I was running out of options. "I am from the USA," I yelled, "see my flag?" (I had been reading Acts all summer, and maybe I was thinking of Paul using his Roman citizenship in Philippi.) Of course, it does not matter what flag you are flying when posing such imminent danger to the US Navy.

"I am alone," I pleaded. "Under these conditions, it will take me a long time to take down the sails."

"Take your time," they said. So I did. Tethered on, fighting wind and waves, I finally managed to take down all the sails under the watchful eyes of the Coast Guard. Then, instead of heading back to where I had begun two hours earlier, I "hove to," which is a way of setting sails and rudder to just drift slowly downwind.

"When can I proceed?"

"Eleven o'clock."

Then we just sat there for hours, the Turkish Coast Guard and *SailingActs,* looking at each other. At exactly eleven o'clock I caught the wind again. The Coast Guard vessel roared off in the other direction. I had just experienced *Mare Nostrum.*

CHAPTER 4

POTENTIAL: THE SEA IN THE GOSPELS

"One day he got into a boat with his disciples, and he said to them, 'Let us go across to the other side of the lake.' So they put out."
Luke 8:22

The people of Judea did not have to travel to Rome to recognize its peril—or its potential. Rome was now a permanent resident of the Land, with Roman soldiers on the roads; Roman architecture in Jerusalem; Roman coins with the emperor's image being circulated; and Greek being acquired, spoken, and resented in the streets.

Rome's seaborne domination was on display on land and sea. The thoroughly pagan city of Caesarea Maritima was the toehold of Rome for reaching the rest of Judea. There Herod had built a harbor, completely artificial. The underwater concrete remains poured two thousand years ago can still be seen.[1] Herod's palace, built out into the sea itself, and the theater facing west toward Rome across the

1. Robert L. Hohlfelder, "Caesarea Maritima: Herod the Great's City on the Sea," *National Geographic* 171 (1987): 260–79. This popularly written article gives a graphic overview of Herod's magnificent achievement of both connecting Judea to Rome and bringing Rome to Judea.

waves were designed to prove to the Jews of Judea that Rome could re-create the world in its own image. Rome ruled the Mediterranean Sea and, because of that, the Mediterranean world, including the little land promised to Abraham and his descendants. The Promised Land was now a province of the Roman Empire. Herod had brought the reality of this triumph of Rome to the Land of Israel.

JEWISH TRAVEL BY SEA IN THE FIRST CENTURY

With the gateways to Rome more open in Judea than ever before, and with thriving Jewish communities growing in the great port cities like Alexandria and Antioch on the Orontes River and many others all around the Mediterranean, Jewish travel was on the rise.[2] But not for everyone. Long-distance travelers, even in the first century AD, were those who were willing to take the risks of losing their privacy, their purity, and perhaps even their lives.

With the spread of Hellenism, by the beginning of the first century, Jewish and gentile people living around the Mediterranean ports were being connected, and influence of Hellenism grew. New challenges to maintaining the religious and cultural distinctions required by the rabbinic kosher laws grew as well. These laws, developed within the context of the Land, were difficult enough to observe there and were nearly impossible to keep at sea. The increasing realities of mobility and social interactions between Jews and gentiles brought life-changing shifts to both groups of people. The varieties of involvement of seaport Jews within broader Hellenized society reached their peak around the shorelines and diminished as one moved further inland, leaving stark differences in the ways inland Jews perceived seagoing

2. I am indebted for the research on Jewish travel in the first-century Mediterranean to the excellent work of one of my graduate students, Eric Trinka, for part of his graduate study program at Eastern Mennonite Seminary. His unpublished 2012 paper "To Sea or Not to Sea? That Is the Question: Jewish Perceptions of Seafaring in Ancient Palestine" is a succinct summary of Jewish seafaring in the first century AD.

peoples.[3] The studies by Catherine Hezser demonstrate the difficulty of adjusting to growing opportunities and threats of traveling by sea, especially to the Jews of Judea.[4]

There had to be compelling reasons to travel, reasons that were strong enough to counteract the deep attachment to the Land of Israel and proximity to the temple in Jerusalem. The most observant Jews likely did not have them. Even most of the non-Jewish population living around the Mediterranean in antiquity did not travel by sea if there were other good options. Merchants, men on official business, people seeking employment, and soldiers traveled by sea. Individual travelers with compelling personal reasons, such as philosophers, teachers, and artists, could be found on ships and walking the land routes. While Jewish people were to be found in all of these categories, the most observant were probably not.[5]

Although most references to Jewish encounters with the people of the Mediterranean are often negative in Hebrew Scripture, some Jewish travel by ship is mentioned (Jonah) or assumed. Judea is connected by ship for trade during Solomon's reign. Ezekiel also includes Israel in the catalog of trade with Tyre. It is in the context of risks and

---

3. This is still the case. For instance, Tel Aviv, on the coast of Israel, is home to a more liberal, secular, hedonistic Jewish population than Jerusalem, with its much higher percentage of ultraorthodox neighborhoods and general public enforcement of rabbinical laws. Our experience of the seaport culture in seaports such as Antalya, Marmaris, and Bodrum, Turkey, was like visiting another country by traveling only a few miles inland. We could order alcohol in most of the waterfront restaurants and even purchase pork in some shops in the seaports, something very rare in inland towns.

4. Catherine Hezser, *Jewish Travel in Antiquity* (Tübingen: Mohr Siebeck, 2011).

5. What about Jesus' denunciation of the Pharisees? "Woe to you, scribes and Pharisees, hypocrites! For you cross sea and land to make a single convert, and you make the new convert twice as much a child of hell as yourselves" (Matt 23:15). While this is a clear denunciation of the zealous attempt to persuade and perhaps pressure others to join the sect of the Pharisees, there is no source outside of the text in Matthew indicating that Pharisees engaged in "overseas" mission. Jesus' words here are more likely hyperbole to emphasize the point. This is the case made by Cohen: "There is absolutely no evidence whatever for missionary activity by the Jews in Egypt, Syria or Asia Minor." Shaye J. D. Cohen, "Did Ancient Jews Missionize," *Biblical Review* 19 (2003): 44.

benefits that "from early times, Judaism probably adopted an ambivalent approach to maritime affairs."[6]

The difficult travel conditions, the challenges to maintaining ritual purity and observing dietary laws, and the lack of privacy and control make the New Testament shift of attitude toward the sea by Jewish followers of Jesus so exceptional. But while it is apparent that Jewish travel by sea for economic and other nonreligious reasons occurred before the first century, travel by religious Jews aboard pagan ships was avoided if possible. The risks of longer land journeys were chosen over the risks of the unclean ships and the people who used them. Nadav Kashtan notes, "Seafaring was ... less attractive for Jews than it was for other groups; seafaring was associated not only with the immediate dangers that any fisherman or navigator may encounter but also with the growing convictions that most enemies of the people of Israel came from the Great Sea."[7]

Despite the resistance to seafaring from the religious leaders of Jerusalem concerned with the threats of Hellenism, its economic and social impacts on the inland population eventually reached unprecedented heights following the time of Alexander's conquests in the East and Greek rule in Palestine. Under the efficiency of Roman occupation, Hellenism offered additional attractions and benefits for those without strong religious or political reasons to resist some assimilation for self-interested reasons. Less-than-observant Jews developed good connections primarily for economic, political, or social-standing purposes. Kashtan observes, "It seems that Jewish involvement in seafaring increased considerably in Judaea under Roman rule as part of the province's political contacts with Rome."[8]

Although the Jews had recently reorganized and had developed a religious identity in the centuries following their Babylonian captivity, Jewish perceptions of the world around them were again challenged

6. Nadav Kashtan, "Seafaring and Jews in Graeco-Roman Palestine: Realistic and Symbolic Dimensions," *Mediterranean Historical Review* 15 (2000): 16.

7. Kashtan, "Seafaring," 18.

8. Kashtan, "Seafaring," 21.

by another and more dominant cultural force—the sea and the Roman Empire that controlled it. For some Jews living in the inland regions that play such a significant role in Greek Scripture—Jerusalem and Galilee—this cultural infiltration brought substantial changes in their ways of thinking and living. Kaftan writes, "The Hellenization and later Romanization of Palestine and the special role of the coastal cities offered the Jews new possibilities and renewed consciousness of the sea."[9]

By the beginning of the first century AD, the necessity of implementing new ways of resisting the influence of the seaborne pagan culture of the Greco-Roman occupiers led to the creation of new social and religious structures. New sea-specific rabbinic teaching was needed. Kashtan explains that the negative "attitude towards maritime activity, with its biblical roots, remained in the collective memory of later Judaism and was formalized in the Talmud by legal prohibitions concerning the impurity of the sea and limits put on long-distance sailing and certain maritime professions."[10] Ritual purity was at stake. Seafaring remained unavoidably unclean. New ways of participating in the unclean pagan world while maintaining purity distinctions were needed, so structures redefining Jewish interactions with gentile peoples living in the diaspora were defined.

On the front lines of this cultural shift were those members of Jewish society who encountered the empire through the seaports—the gateways to water travel and trade to the ends of the earth. But the seafarers with whom Hellenized Jews and, subsequently, Judean Jews came into contact were in a multitude of ways seen as ritually unclean. Although Jewish religious society had established significant interactions with seafaring cultures as recorded in Scripture, times had most definitely changed. The connections of King Solomon to the seafaring culture of Tyre had been attractive for mutually beneficial reasons such as trade. And although cultural assimilation was

9. Kashtan, "Seafaring," 17.

10. Kashtan, "Seafaring," 18.

risky, its threat was limited. The invasions of seafaring Greeks or the recent waves of Roman conquests in Palestine posed a much greater threat, a clearer and more present danger. As a Roman province, the sea became an unavoidable aspect of interacting with Rome.[11]

With the rising level of cultural assimilation brought by the continuous Roman presence in the Land of Israel, differences of opinion inevitably arose in the discussion of Jewish relationships with the resident seafarers. Among the Jewish leaders and the population, various opposing sects emerged seeking to engage the new political domination of Rome in different ways, pushing and pulling Hellenized and observant Jews in different directions. These sects constantly debated how to adjust to the reality of Roman occupation while maintaining fidelity to God and preserving their distinct identity as God's people. The rewards for cooperation with Rome and the consequences for noncooperation—which the Romans publicly reinforced—heightened the stakes. Under these circumstances, preexisting disagreements within the Jewish society were exacerbated, driving wedges further into a Jewish psyche that was already divided both politically and religiously. Soon the splintering sects of Jewish society would have to make decisions regarding their constituencies' participation in seafaring culture. An alternative, theologically based argument for Jewish participation in seafaring would become a central issue in Greek Scripture.

In the first century, those Jews from Judea who did travel were likely less concerned about religious purity, Sabbath observance, and diet—all of which posed significant problems—than those who refused to travel for religious reasons. Hezser describes the challenges:

> One had to reckon with long waiting periods in foreign ports, with times of hunger and thirst on the open sea, and the possibility that one's life was put into jeopardy if the captain was reckless. Individual travelers, even if they were Roman officials,

11. Kashtan, "Seafaring," 20.

> had little control over the hazards that accompanied ship journeys. They were utterly dependent on the ship's captain and crew, whose foremost concerns were economic and who would have cared more for themselves, their ships, and their merchandise than for the passengers they carried.[12]

We will return to the problem of travel for deeply religious Jews in the Acts story.[13]

While detailed evidence of Jewish participation in sea travel is rather scarce across the broad span of history, it is plausible from the historical records of literary sources and a limited number of artifacts dating to the time of the Hebrew Scriptures that there was indeed a limited level of participation by Jews in maritime society. Hezser's study of changing Jewish travel practices in the context of the Greco-Roman "culture of mobility" indicates that rabbinic commentary on the challenges of sea travel for observant Jews became more common after the first century, following the destruction of Jerusalem.[14] Later writings from the Talmudic period document the prevailing opinions about sea travel from the perspective of a Jerusalem-based elite. These writings also document a later shift from a rejection of seafaring culture to toleration and mitigation of its uncleanliness for the purposes of trade and religiously stipulated travel. But this is not yet the case in the first century during the time of Acts and the remainder of the Greek New Testament.

---

12. Hezser, *Jewish Travel*, 165.

13. The dilemma posed to observant Jews living in Israel even today who would like to sail with us on *SailingActs* helps me appreciate the difficulty of being in the completely nonkosher environment of a sailboat with a Christian owner and crew, comparable to the situation for Jews interested in sea travel in the first century. My wife and I have had long conversations with some friends who are very observant Jews living in Israel. We had stayed in their home many times with no problems, for we joined fully into their customs, diet, and schedule. However, it proved to be far more difficult for them to join us sailing. While it looked possible, it was extremely challenging to find solutions to accommodate the kosher requirements. It would have meant their bringing with them all the food and utensils necessary for a strictly kosher diet. And that was only the beginning.

14. Catherine Hezser, "Travel and Mobility," in *Oxford Handbook for Jewish Daily Life in Roman Palestine*, ed. Catherine Hezser (Oxford: Oxford University Press, 2010), 210–26.

With the Greek New Testament, a world-changing shift of focus from land to sea, from the Promised Land to the entire planet, begins. The Greek New Testament is the dramatic chart of the sea routes toward the ends of the earth, moving far beyond the new adaptations of rabbinic instructions for faithful Jewish seafaring.

THE SEA OF GALILEE

We begin by looking at the Sea of Galilee in the context of the rural, land-based culture of first-century Judea. The Sea of Galilee is mostly ignored in Hebrew Scripture, twice referred to as "the sea of Chinnereth" (יָם כִּנֶּרֶת, *yām kinneret*) as a tribal boundary marker (Num 34:11; Josh 13:27). In terms of travel, it is insignificant—until Jesus.

At a time when the trading and navy ships were plying the waters of the Mediterranean in record numbers, the armies were marching along the roads, the seaports were accumulating staggering wealth, and huge social tensions were occurring within the Jewish community because of these seafaring activities, Jesus was born in a land of shepherds and farmers. Once a glorious independent kingdom, it was then a small, occupied province of Rome, the greatest sea empire the world had ever known. Beyond prayers and hope, there seemed to be few realistic options for independence. Cooperation and resistance both had consequences.

The profound transition from land to sea in the biblical story begins with Jesus. For the first time in Scripture, Jesus demonstrates a fundamental change in perception of the sea and its people through the choices he makes in his ministry among the inhabitants around the rim of the Sea of Galilee. Like sea waves against the cliffs, Jesus' actions begin to erode the land-centric assumptions of his followers and the perspective from Jerusalem toward the sea and its people.

The contrast of the perspective of the Greek New Testament writers with that of the writers of Hebrew Scripture and Greek Apocrypha is nothing less than revolutionary. Jesus uses boats. He calls seafarers. Parables of the kingdom of God include the sea. Jesus is the ruler of the Sea of Galilee even if Rome controls it. The stories of the sea in the Gospels describe and demonstrate the opportunities and risks of the sea, but never the rejection of it for self-preservation. The gospel travels by land and sea to the people of land and sea.

Nazareth, the small village that was home to Jesus, likely for most of his life, is located about halfway between the Mediterranean Sea to the west and the Sea of Galilee to the east. But although Nazareth is landlocked, Jesus certainly could see the Mediterranean by climbing the short, steep hike to the top of the Nazareth Ridge. From there, the Mediterranean is clearly visible. Jesus could even have spotted the sails of the coastal cargo ships making their way from Tyre to Caesarea and beyond. Jesus, growing up as normal for children in Nazareth and any other village, "increasing in wisdom and stature, and in favor with God and men" (Luke 2:52 NASB), demonstrates from the limited account of his childhood an above-average curiosity, insight, and imagination.[15] What does he conclude about the world by gazing out at the seagoing ships from far away that he sees from Nazareth Ridge?

At the same time that Jesus was growing up in Nazareth, the Roman-style town of Sepphoris, about four miles (6 km) from Nazareth, was being expanded and developed with impressive Roman architecture. The city was also visible from the Nazareth Ridge. Jesus would never go to Rome, but Rome was in his neighborhood in Galilee. There is even the possibility that when Jesus was old enough to work alongside his father, he would have accompanied him to work in Sepphoris.[16]

15. The story of Jesus in the Jerusalem temple at age twelve demonstrates this clearly. According to Luke's account, Jesus had stayed behind in the temple, where his parents found him "sitting among the teachers, listening to them and asking them questions" (Luke 2:46). This gives incredible insight into the kind of youth Jesus was. But that is not all: "All who heard [Jesus] were amazed at his understanding and his answers" (Luke 2:47).

16. While this is speculative, the necessity for Joseph to earn some income beyond the meager sources available in Nazareth would have taken Joseph to places where he could use his skill as a craftsman or builder. Jesus would have been expected to help.

But Jesus did not go toward the Mediterranean Sea coast and its ports connected to the rest of the world or remain in Nazareth.[17] He based his ministry in Capernaum, a small fishing village on the north end of the Sea of Galilee. Why did he base his ministry there?

During his ministry around the Sea of Galilee, the Roman city of Tiberias, complete with baths, theater, and temples, was prominent. Constructed around AD 18–20 by Herod Antipas, son of Herod the Great, the building project must have been one of the most impressive sites to observe and discuss among the Jewish population living near the Sea and fishing its waters. It was made the capital of Galilee under Herod Antipas and was such a dominating presence in the entire region that John's Gospel twice refers to the Sea of Galilee as "the Sea of Tiberias" (Τιβεριάδος, *Tiberiados*; John 6:1; 21:1). Yet Jesus does not mention Tiberias even once in the Gospels. The Roman city of Tiberias, named after the Roman emperor, is not relevant to Jesus' agenda. The Jewish Capernaum, the "village of Nahum" the Hebrew prophet, however, is.

From the point of view of the Hebrew writers, the Sea of Galilee itself is irrelevant. This changes with Jesus. The Sea of Galilee is mentioned in Scripture by this name for the first time by the Gospel writers. Jesus invites people who live near the Sea of Galilee to follow him. Some of these people are fishermen who make their living on the Sea of Galilee. They sail its waters daily, selling their fish to Jews as well as pagans who also live around the sea. In the Gospels, fishermen are featured as central figures in the ministry of Jesus. At least one of the writers of the Gospels is a fisherman himself. The fishermen disciples tell the sea stories that they and Jesus are in, for amazingly, Jesus himself uses boats. Jesus is the first Hebrew prophet recorded in Scripture since Jonah to use boats, albeit for precisely the opposite reason from Jonah.

17. It should be noted that Nazareth was not isolated. The *Via Maris*, the main route between the eastern interior and the Mediterranean seaports, ran through the Jezreel Valley just below Nazareth. The boy Jesus could easily have observed the movement of Roman soldiers, people, and goods from the hill overlooking the valley. Nazareth would have given the young Jesus an awareness of the world, connected by land and sea.

The Gospel writers' sea vocabulary gives insight into the shift from Hebrew to Greek in awareness of the sea. The Greek word used by Matthew, Mark, and John—but not Luke—for the Sea of Galilee is "sea" (θάλασσα, *thalassa*). This is the same word that Luke uses for the Mediterranean. But Luke, knowing a sea when he sees one, calls the Galilee a "lake" (λίμνη, *limnē*). The difference between Luke's technical vocabulary and the other Gospel writers' rather limited and general nautical vocabulary demonstrates that although they are familiar with boats and water, their awareness of the Mediterranean Sea and the traditions and language of the seafaring Greeks is very limited. Table 2 below demonstrates the frequency and terminology of the Gospel writers' references to the Sea of Galilee.

TABLE 2: **Frequency and terms for the Sea of Galilee used by the Gospel writers**

Gospel	Term Used	Number of Occurrences
Matthew	Sea (θάλασσα, *thalassa*)	14
Mark	Sea (θάλασσα, *thalassa*)	17
Luke	Lake (λίμνη, *limnē*)	5
John	Sea (θάλασσα, *thalassa*)	9

The geographical features and the political divisions of the Sea of Galilee are extremely important to appreciate the sea-shaped dynamics of Jesus' ministry that have so many immediate and long-term implications for Jesus' followers. This lake, almost seven hundred feet (about 200 m) below sea level, is the world's lowest freshwater lake. Only the Dead Sea has a lower altitude on the entire planet.[18] It is small, measuring a mere twelve miles (19 km) north to south at its longest point, and about eight miles (13 km) east to west at its widest. From any point on or around the lake, the entire rim is visible.

18. I do not think it is of any theological or missiological importance that Jesus did most of his ministry below sea level, but it is a rather startling fact considering that mountains and high places are important both in Judaism and Canaanite religions.

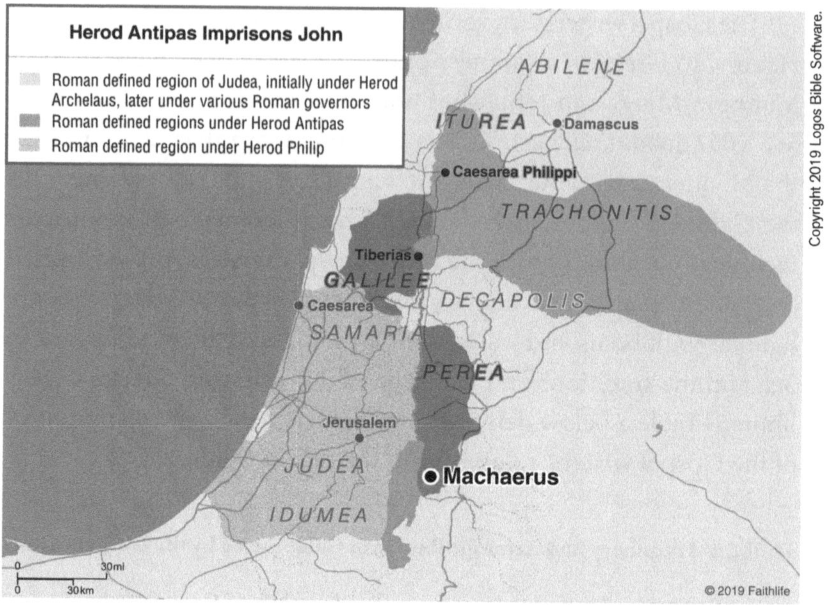

MAP 2: **The sea that connects diversity**

The political divisions add to the uniqueness. On map 2 the three administrative districts can be located. Galilee on the western side of the lake, with the city of Tiberias strategically positioned for control, is mostly Jewish, with some Hellenistic areas, and is administered by Herod Antipas. Capernaum is in Galilee. Phillip's Territory, or Gaulanitis, on the northeast section of the Sea, is governed by Herod Philip. This area has mixed Jewish and Hellenistic influences. Bethsaida is located in this territory, as is Caesarea Philippi with its pagan temple.[19] Finally, Decapolis on the southeastern quarter of the sea is a "bastion of Hellenism and Roman imperial might, established

19. There is some dispute on the exact location of Bethsaida. Two possible locations are el-Aradj, the fishing harbor on the shore, and et-Tell, the village located some distance from the sea. For a summary of the evidence for both et-Tell and El-Aradj being the Bethsaida of the Gospels, see Steven R. Notley and Mordechai Aviam, "Searching for Bethsaida: The Case for El-Araj," *Biblical Archaeology Review* 46 (2020): 28–39. For an earlier work arguing for et-Tell, see Rami Arav et al., "Bethsaida Rediscovered," *Biblical Archaeology Review* 26 (2000): 44–51, 53–56.

to guard Rome's eastern frontier."[20] Scythopolis (present-day Beit She'an), also with temples, baths, and theater, is located here.

In its connected diversity, the Sea of Galilee is kind of a miniature Mediterranean Sea. Its little ports around the entire rim connected the diversity of people of the "Galilee of the nations" (Isa 9:1) described by Isaiah as "the people who walked in darkness" (Isa 9:2). Is this variety of people, with easy connections by boat, the reason Jesus chooses the town of Capernaum? And does he call fishermen to his inner circle of disciples because they are seafarers with connections to the people around the lake? Are there other reasons for Jesus coming to the Sea of Galilee?[21]

Jewish fishermen are rare in Jewish literature. They are not mentioned in the Hebrew Scriptures. In the first century, fishermen were regarded as having very low status, for they were perpetually unclean from the unclean fish they had to handle. They did business with pagans living around the eastern side of the sea and especially the southern end. Roman authorities and those who collected Rome's taxes mistrusted fishermen because with their boats they could avoid paying border taxes when crossing the territorial boundaries that divided the perimeter of the Sea of Galilee—for instance, when crossing between Capernaum and Bethsaida. The mistrust between the Roman authorities and the fishermen was mutual. And Jesus chooses fishermen.

It bears repeating that Jesus is the first Hebrew prophet who used boats to be featured in Scripture since Jonah, but whereas Jonah boarded a ship headed toward Tarshish to avoid taking God's message to the pagans of Nineveh, Jesus used boats to take God's message

20. Paul Wright, *Understanding the New Testament: An Introductory Atlas* (Jerusalem: Carta, 2004), 23.

21. Shelly Wachsman, the marine archeologist who led the excavation of the ancient Galilee boat (or Jesus Boat) discovered near Kibbutz Ginnosar in 1986, raises the possibility that Jesus may have had previous connections. "Perhaps Jesus was drawn to the lake because he had already spent time on the Kinneret during the missing years of his young adulthood. If so, might Jesus have worked as a carpenter, perhaps building boats on the lake during that time?" Shelly Wachsman, *The Sea of Galilee Boat* (College Station, TX: Texas A&M University Press, 2009), 352.

FIGURE 8: **And they left their nets and followed**

to everyone, including the pagans from Rome. Jesus seems to have recognized the advantages of a boat- and sea-based ministry. The Sea of Galilee is the center of a network of relationships across clear geographical and cultural boundaries, relative cultural openness because of these relationships despite the boundaries, and efficiency of travel among the diverse groups of people around the rim of the Sea.

For the remainder of the New Testament, the Sea of Galilee is mentioned only in connection with Jesus and his followers. Jesus puts the Sea of Galilee on the biblical map, making it, despite its size and its being practically irrelevant in Hebrew Scripture, the most famous lake in the world. The boat and storm-ending dramas have no precedent in Scripture. This is remarkable for several reasons given that storm stories are much more common in Greek literature and the records of Roman seafaring. Storms at sea in antiquity, especially with Greek seafarers, are associated with the whims of the gods, be they wrath or blessing. Sea, seafaring, boats, storms, the Roman domination of the seas, and the occupation of Judea are all problematic or negative to the people of Galilee. The amount of story time the New Testament gives to the description of events on the waters of the Sea of Galilee is completely revolutionary compared with the Hebrew Scriptures. Why?

Seas, even familiar little ones, are beyond human control. Even the tiny Sea of Galilee can terrorize fishermen who have grown up sailing their little boats on its waters. Luke was not in the boat those nights when Peter, James, and John thought they were going to die, but getting swamped in an open boat will terrify anyone, and those disciples in the boat who survived that night told and retold the story for the rest of their lives to incredulous audiences.

The Sea of Galilee might not be big like the Mediterranean, but it can kill you just as quickly. When it is storming, the Sea of Galilee is a *sea*. There are two storm stories in the Gospels. The conditions of both sudden, unexpected squalls coming from either the west or the east are realistic, causing the kind of waves that can easily swamp small, open boats. In the first storm story, Jesus is aboard sleeping, wakes up, and calms the storm (Matt 8:24–27; Mark 4:35–41; Luke 8:22–25). In the second story, at about three or four in the morning, Jesus is not aboard but arrives by foot on the water just before the disciples in the sinking boat, near exhaustion from bailing and rowing, give up (Matt 14:22–33; Mark 6:45–51; John 6:17–21). The sea has become a dreadful place. Sinking sailors, even Jesus' disciples, see ghosts and other horrible creatures more clearly when their eyes and minds are freed from rational thought. So, when the disciples see something on the water coming toward them, their imaginations go to work. "A ghost!" Up to twelve desperate men, among them several seasoned Galilee seafarers, call out in the anguish only those who are perishing understand.

Aside from the story of Jonah, there is nothing else like these two sea stories in Scripture. What is the significance of these stories? Are the disciples aware of the popular claim among Roman subjects that Caesar Augustus has dominion over storms at sea? "Who then is this," they exclaim in awe, "that even the wind and the sea obey him?" (Mark 4:41).

Jesus' final words to his disciples on the Mount of Olives as they look out over Jerusalem indicate a profound shift from land to sea, not only geographically but missiologically and theologically as well. The shock and consternation of the disciples, while not described, are implied in their actions as Jesus is taken up from their sight. Jerusalem, the center of the Jewish conceptual and religious world, was dangerous. While they understood that they would need to stay in Jerusalem until they received the gift promised by Jesus, they had no idea how long they would have to wait for it (Acts 1:4–8). So being "witnesses" in Judea likely sounded a little less threatening. Following Jesus through Samaria had been confusing, and perhaps unpleasant, but not especially dangerous. But Jesus does not end there. His final instructions end with "the ends of the earth" (Acts 1:8). These final words of Jesus are likely especially terrifying to the disciples, feeling vulnerable and uncertain, hearing them on the Mount of Olives. And then Jesus leaves them.

THE SEA CHANGE IN SCRIPTURE

The Gospel writers' use of sea language in the New Testament indicates their primary location and identity with "sea" in contrast with the land-centric identity of the Hebrew writers. It is not that they refer to the sea more often; it is their perspective on and familiarity with the sea that have significance.

The Greek word *thalassa* ("sea") appears ninety-two times in the Greek New Testament and is translated each time as "sea" in the KJV. In the Gospels, Matthew, Mark, and John all use *thalassa* for the Sea of Galilee. While Luke uses *thalassa* three times in his Gospel, it is always referring to the Mediterranean. Luke refers to "Lake (*limnē*)

Galilee" five times. *Thalassa* and *limnē* together are used forty-three times by the Gospel writers—twenty-nine times descriptively or neutrally, nine times negatively when recounting the storm episodes, and five times when Jesus demonstrates his power over the sea. In addition, Matthew refers to the Mediterranean three times, Mark twice, and Luke three times. John does not mention the Mediterranean at all in his Gospel.

The Red Sea appears fifty-eight times in nine books of the Hebrew Scriptures and four times in the Greek New Testament, not being mentioned in the Gospels at all. The seas where God's power is displayed are the Sea of Galilee and the Mediterranean Sea. These seas are important in the present and the future, rather than the past.

As can be expected, Luke uses *thalassa* a total of seven times, only describing action near or on the Mediterranean. Luke quotes others who are using *thalassa* generically as part of creation and once, in quoting Stephen's final speech before the Rabbinic Council, when he mentions the Red Sea in Acts 7.

The Epistle writers use *thalassa* a total of ten times, with only Paul making a general reference to the Mediterranean Sea, once in 2 Corinthians 11:26 as one of the dangers he faced. The Red Sea is mentioned four times, twice by name, and referenced twice descriptively. The writer of Revelation uses *thalassa* more than any other New Testament writer both literally and metaphorically. We will examine the writer's use of "sea" in Revelation more closely in the final chapter.

The general pattern in the New Testament, then, continues to connect to the sea stories in the Hebrew Scriptures and the reference to the sea as a metaphor for both blessings and evil. But in contrast to the Hebrew Scripture, the majority of references to the sea in the Greek New Testament involve personal experiences of the writers and observations of others—Jews and gentiles, landlubbers and seafarers—on or near the Sea of Galilee and the Mediterranean.

The Sea of Galilee is described by the writers of the Gospels much as the Mediterranean Sea is depicted by the writers of the Hebrew Scriptures. In both cases, the sea and its people are presented realistically, as are the seas themselves. There are natural and human perils along with natural and human positive potential. The difference is the participation of the writers.

TRANSITION

Following Pentecost, the movement in Acts is relentlessly toward the Mediterranean Sea. Paul, born in the seaport of Tarsus and then radicalized in Jerusalem as a zealot guardian of the Law, is a man of land and sea, Hellenist and Pharisee, Jew and Greek. What Jesus had begun on the Sea of Galilee, Paul and the early Christians continue on and around the Mediterranean Sea. While Hebrew Scriptures focus almost exclusively on the Land and its people, Luke's writing not only includes but focuses with clarity and accurate nautical terminology on the sea and its people. The writers themselves, whether on the Sea of Galilee or the Mediterranean, are in the stories they write, as increasingly are the Jewish and Greek followers of Jesus. These seas not only connect the story of Jesus to the rest of humanity anywhere in the world, but the story of God's people in Scripture now *includes* all people, landlubbers and seafarers alike. The Mediterranean is now the sea of history and Scripture, of the Roman Empire, and of the kingdom of God.

Beginning in Acts, and especially with Paul, the sea in Scripture becomes the Scripture in the sea. The remainder of Scripture now will mostly be written by, about, and to seafarers. Because of this, it is written to us, for we have inherited and inhabit that Mediterranean-shaped world as well.[22]

---

22. Luke uses around forty-eight different Greek nautical terms in Luke and Acts that the other New Testament writers do not use. Only two of these unique nautical terms appear in Luke. While other New Testament writers use nautical terms, Luke's usage is more technical and more precise, and his descriptions are verifiably accurate. This demonstrates Luke's familiarity with all things related to sailing on the Mediterranean, far beyond that of any other writer of Hebrew or Greek Scripture. The vocabulary of Luke in his Gospel and Acts demonstrates a major shift of vocabulary in Scripture. The first example in Acts recounts the vision of Peter seeing the "sheet" from heaven (Acts 10:11). The Greek word ὀθόνη (*othonē*) can be translated as "linen cloth," implying a sail. About ninety percent of the nautical terms used only by Luke

REFLECTIONS FROM THE SEA

We spent our first winter aboard *SailingActs* in Ashkelon. Local fishermen had occupied one corner of the marina. They did not mingle with any of the sailors. They had their own tight-knit fraternity, it seemed, and their schedule of leaving the marina at dusk to fish all night and then returning in the early morning did not match the schedules of the live-aboard sailors, who tended to sleep at night. Very early each morning, the fishermen would congregate loudly on "their" dock, cleaning fish, mending nets, and shouting in Hebrew.

I was intrigued by these Jewish fishermen mending their nets and keeping to themselves. We had made a short visit to our home in the United States over Christmas, and Janet had decided to stay a bit longer. The solitude of being alone aboard *SailingActs* back in Ashkelon, I reasoned, would be an excellent opportunity to work full-time on a writing project. The hermit-writing progressed nicely; my social interactions withered. Maybe I could try to talk to the fishermen, I thought one particularly long afternoon when I had run out of writing energy. Maybe I could get some insight into what it is like to be a fisherman, and maybe that would help me understand those fishermen on the Sea of Galilee. I learned more than I was expecting.

I grabbed my camera, approached the fishermen mending their nets, and in very polite sign language asked if I could take their photo. "*LO! LO!*" ("no, no"). I do not give up easily, so in very friendly broken Hebrew I managed "me friend," "everything good," "pictures only for me," and so forth.

No progress at all. I knew better than to push this too far and had begun to meekly retreat when suddenly, from down the dock, the boss fishman came charging at me. "*LO!*" He shouted, "You from tax?"

And then it hit me. They were thinking maybe I was some kind of sneaky, undercover official, that I was there to document something

---

appear in Acts 27 and 28, describing the details of Paul's voyage to Rome. See the appendix for a list of nautical terms used only by Luke in Scripture.

like tax fraud or perhaps spy on their possible smuggling operations. So I backed away having learned far more about the Sea of Galilee fishermen than I had anticipated or hoped.

That day helped me understand the disciples, leaving their nets to follow Jesus. For they, like the fishermen disciples of Jesus, were marginalized from polite society and were suspicious of authority, especially tax collectors. And perhaps because of that, they did not have so much to lose by following Jesus when he invited them. Except there was a problem. Another kind of marginalized Jew, a tax collector, was also invited. And he joined too!

CHAPTER 5

COMPETITION: *MARE NOSTRUM* AND ACTS

"So, being sent out by the Holy Spirit,
they went down to Seleucia;
and from there they sailed to Cyprus."
Acts 13:4

The disciples of Jesus lost their fear of the Mediterranean Sea and its people at Pentecost. Jesus had set the stage for connecting to the "ends of the earth" by water on the tiny Galilee. Their experience with the storms of the Galilee, along with Jesus' presence in those storms, had likely increased their confidence in sailing and connecting to all of the diverse population around the lake, but the leaving-Jerusalem part of Jesus' instructions to be his witnesses to the ends of the earth by land and (Mediterranean) sea was another matter. As described in the previous chapter, observant Judean Jews did not like to sail on the Mediterranean.

The story in Acts moves immediately toward the seaports of *Mare Nostrum*—the gateways to the ends of the earth. Further progress westward required the help of Hellenized, seafaring Jewish believers in Jesus. The people of the land and the sea, Jew and Greek, monotheist and pagan, landlubber and seafarer increasingly share the same space in the story in Acts and the instructions in the Epistles. Recognizing the deep aversion of observant Judean Jews to travel by sea helps us to appreciate the kind of radical courage that representatives of the early Christian movement in the Mediterranean, especially non-Hellenized Jews like Peter, needed to travel on land and sea.

Following the gift of the Holy Spirit, the promised power immediately results in the disciples and their fellow believers following the instructions of Jesus—moving from Jerusalem on to Judea and Samaria and, very shortly thereafter, on to the ends of the earth. The ends of the earth, from the Judean perspective, begin at the shores of the Mediterranean. Long the toehold of enemies like the Philistines, Phoenicians, and empires that controlled the *Via Maris* that followed the coast, the seaports were bases of Roman control and symbols of Greco-Roman cultural domination.

THE SEA CHANGE

The shift from the Sea of Galilee to the Mediterranean Sea is a biblical sea change that impacts the message of the gospel, the inclusion of pagans in the promises of the kingdom, theology, ecclesiology, the development of Western civilization, and world history. This shift begins, not with a bang, but rather with a kind of whimper from the disciples hoping for the promised kingdom immediately. They are on the Mount of Olives overlooking the Temple Mount and the city of Jerusalem where Jesus had been arrested and crucified only weeks before. They ask, "Lord, is this the time when you will restore the kingdom to Israel?" (Acts 1:6). Jesus did not answer their question chronologically but geographically. "You will receive power when the Holy Spirit has come upon you," Jesus promises, "and you will be my witnesses in Jerusalem and in all Judea and Samaria, and to the end of the earth" (Acts 1:8). Then he leaves them to get over the shock.[1]

1. How did the disciples understand the ending words of Jesus' sending mandate? Was Jesus connecting this phrase to Isaiah's prediction of the light of salvation reaching to the "end(s) of the earth" (Isa 49:6; 52:10) with a universal inference or a specific geographical location? I do

JERUSALEM AND JUDEA

What follows immediately in Acts 2, beginning in Jerusalem with the "storm" of the Holy Spirit's arrival,[2] is a geographical fulfillment of Jesus' prediction. Beginning in the temple of Jerusalem with Peter's healing of the beggar, followed by such dramatic, revolutionary words and actions of the followers of Jesus, the entire city of Jerusalem, and likely all Judea as well, hears the news. The movements from Jerusalem toward Judea, Samaria, and the ends of the earth are recorded in rapid succession in the first eleven chapters of the Acts story.

The feast of Pentecost was one of the three annual pilgrimage festivals when adult Jewish males were required to worship at the temple in Jerusalem. For the Jews living throughout the empire, scattered as they were around the Mediterranean, travel to Judea presented severe challenges, especially if coming by sea.

In the first century, as is the case even today in the Mediterranean, the sailing season begins in May and ends in late October. The months

---

not believe Jesus was limiting his mandate to a specific geographical region. There are several reasons for this. One, Luke is likely a Greek seafarer. It seems more likely that the disciples were not thinking of a specific geographical location. Although biblical scholars tend to think in terms of land geography, routes, and destinations, sea geography is unlimited. Two, at the seaport of Caesarea, where Peter finds himself in the house of Cornelius (Acts 10), they are connected to the ends of the earth. The ends of the earth begin at the seaports. Three, the next recorded locations of the Christians are primarily sea-connected geographic locations—Phoenicia, Cyprus, and Antioch. When seafarers face the sea from a seaport, the "ends of the earth" are not specific geographic locations but everywhere they can potentially go. It is seafarers, with an experience-based view of seafaring, either on the Galilee or the Mediterranean, who are the primary emissaries and recipients of the rest of the Acts story. The Greek outward-looking, limitless view of the world based on their sea perspective seems to be how the seaport-born, seafaring Barnabas and Saul of Tarsus understood and began to carry out the mission mandate of Jesus toward the west. Eckard J. Schnabel believes that "the ends of the earth" can be understood in a general, metaphorical sense, implying the worldwide mission mandate, but states, "It is preferable to interpret the phrase 'end(s) of the earth' as a geographical term as well." Eckard J. Schnabel, "Jesus' Missionary Commission and the Ends of the Earth," in *Lexham Geographic Commentary on Acts through Revelation*, ed. Barry J. Beitzel (Bellingham, WA: Lexham Press, 2019), 51–56. This volume is an excellent resource on the historical and geographical context of the Christian movement westward. I agree that the "ends of the earth" can best be understood in an unlimited geographical sense to include the known and unknown world.

2. The description of Pentecost with the powerful wind creating conditions of a storm at sea, so familiar to Peter and some of the others, is a remarkable initiation and a predictive metaphor of the seafaring nature of navigating to the ends of the earth with the gospel.

between are prone to severe winter storms. Passover, the first of the three pilgrimage festivals, was celebrated in the spring, a little early for safe and reliable ship transportation to Judea for the Jewish communities in the diaspora.[3] The festival of Succoth, or the Feast of Tabernacles, was celebrated in the fall, too late in the sailing season to risk sea travel. Pentecost, fifty days after Passover, was, and still is, generally during optimal sailing weather, and indeed, this pilgrimage festival drew the highest numbers of Jews living around the Mediterranean to Jerusalem. At Pentecost, Jews from the "ends of the earth" were in Jerusalem, a veritable wave of humanity from the empire.[4] The sea enabled many of these Jews to live far from Jerusalem and still fulfill at least part of their pilgrimage obligations.

Peter's address to the gathered Jews of the diaspora, who were more than a little familiar with the power and triumph of Rome, includes references to Jesus' power and triumph in the resurrection. This must have sounded especially shocking to the residents of the empire in Jerusalem for Pentecost, especially when Peter connected Jesus' kingdom to David's in his explanatory, prophetic sermon. The listeners would not soon forget this sermon and would return to their homes in the diaspora to share their experiences and questions within the Jewish communities of the empire. The eyewitness accounts of the Pentecost events, and the explanation of Peter, were almost certainly carried to the "ends of the earth" before the apostles did so.

---

3. We discovered the validity of the ancient advice against sailing in April when in 2005 we departed Ashkelon toward the ancient harbor of Caesarea to begin the long voyage following the route of Paul's journey to Rome. We left in mid-afternoon in a forecasted "good weather window." We had two able-bodied students aboard, so we were pretty confident of the capabilities to sail through the night. But within several hours of leaving Ashkelon, where we had wintered, we were hit with a sudden spring storm in the gathering darkness. It was so violent and uncomfortable, and with the only functioning seaman (me) extremely seasick, we abandoned the plan and took refuge, entering the Herzliya Marina in the stormy darkness to recover for a day.

4. A number of the regions listed in Acts 2:9–11 are linked to Jerusalem by the ports on the Mediterranean Sea. The people from these areas, especially from distant ports like Rome (Acts 2:10), most likely traveled to Israel by sea on ships owned and operated by non-Jews. There were no other good options.

JOPPA, CAESAREA, AND THE ENDS OF THE EARTH

The story of Peter and Cornelius in Acts 10 completes the move toward the sea not just geographically but socially and theologically as well. The story begins with Cornelius, a gentile attracted to Judaism and a centurion of the "Italian Cohort" (Acts 10:1). He is stationed in Caesarea and lives among representatives of Roman rule and various other sea invaders. Peter is in Joppa, another of the very few seaports of the Land of Israel. As Cornelius is being directed to send for Peter in Joppa, Peter is receiving a vision that will prepare him for one of the most important meetings in the history of the nascent Jesus movement. Peter, on the roof of the house, sees "something like a large sheet" (Acts 10:11) coming down from, of all places, *heaven,* full of nonkosher animals.

The details are significant here. Remember, the invasion of the unclean food and practices of the gentiles is seen by the people of Judea to come from the sea, not from heaven. And this sheet, which for modern readers might conjure up images of a bed sheet—something not used in first-century Judea—can be interpreted as a "billowing sail," for the Greek word used in the story, *othonē,* refers either to a linen cloth or to a sail. To think of the sheet as a sail is consistent with the content of the story and descriptive of the square, four-cornered linen sails used in the first century. The vision gets Peter to meet and, reluctantly perhaps, accept Cornelius. But because the vision represents so clearly the sea invasion of the abhorrent Greeks and Romans with their pagan practices and unclean cuisine, it helps the early Christian community, which now includes Hellenistic Jews from seaports, to accept the peoples and cultures of the Mediterranean Sea.

Caesarea, the pagan Roman port city, the gateway to Rome in the land, was built under Herod the Great as an important link to the Roman shipping network. Caesarea honored Rome in its name and architecture. A temple dedicated to Caesar Augustus dominated the harbor. With its theater and hippodrome, Caesarea was a showcase of Roman presence. With Herod's palace and the new artificial harbor built using the recently developed concrete, extending into the water as if reaching for Rome, Caesarea was the base of Roman administration in Judea.[5] Peter, in his visit with Cornelius, is already at the ends of the earth (compare Acts 8:40).

In a matter of four chapters, Acts 8–11, a total of five significant Mediterranean seaports—Gaza, Joppa, Caesarea, Cyprus, and Antioch—are connected to the events of the landlocked city of Jerusalem. This is an incredibly significant turn that sets the stage for the action shifting from Jerusalem to Antioch, the most important seaport on the eastern end of the Mediterranean Sea.

ANTIOCH

The third largest city in the empire on the eastern end of the Mediterranean Sea, thanks to its strategic location, was named by the Greek commander Seleucus, who had served under Alexander the Great. Following the struggle for succession of Alexander's empire, Seleucus established control over a vast portion of the Greek Empire in around 300 BC and named the city after his father, Antiochus.[6] Seleucus made Antioch the capital of the western part of the huge Seleucid Empire, of which Judea was now part. The Seleucid rule ended in Judea with the Roman conquest in 63 BC.[7]

As with the New World of Western history, it was the seafarers who were at the forefront of significant shifts in maps, history, perceptions, and cultures. Seafarers were the eyes and ears of the cultures from which they came, viewing the world for others, making

---

5. For an excellent summary of Caesarea and its construction, features, and importance, see Paul Wright, "The Geography of Caesarea Maritima," in Beitzel, *Lexham Geographic Commentary on Acts through Revelation*, 202–21.

6. This Antioch, known as Syrian Antioch, or Antioch on the Orontes, was not the only city so named. Located in Turkey today, it has the name of Hatay. Another Antioch appears in Acts, the first inland city visited by Paul. It is in Turkey as well and is referred to as "Antioch in Pisidia" (Acts 13:14) and is near the current town of Yalvaç, Turkey.

7. All of the Greek New Testament was written during the time the Romans called their province "Judea." Although the term "Judea" in some form was used by others before and after the Israelites entered the Land, it was not until the rule of Emperor Hadrian (AD 117–38) that Judea became a Roman province designated as "Judea Judea," or simply "Judea." The Jewish inhabitants commonly continued to use the Land of Israel or Judea during the time of the New Testament. Israel, or the Land of Israel, is used by its citizens to this day.

irreversible contact with strangers, introducing these strangers to the ideas and knowledge they had brought with them, and bringing back home the ideas and knowledge from those they had met. Ultimately, these seafaring explorers and traders provided those who sent them with cultural mirrors. This made it possible for the sending cultures to view themselves in new ways. The people living in the seaports of the Mediterranean were at the forefront of this kind of cultural exchange, for they were connected to the world of ideas, religions, philosophies, and the latest news, including "good news."

Sociologist Rodney Stark describes the kinds of people who lived and utilized the urban seaports of the empire around the Mediterranean Sea.[8] These great cities were centers of pluralism. Their inhabitants were open to trading goods and gods, ideas and idols with the rest of the world. It is no surprise to discover that urban seaports were among the earliest cities in which churches were established.

The role of seaports sets the stage for the primary actor in the book of Acts, the apostle to the gentiles, the apostle Paul, who, like other seafarers, utilized the seaports and connected with people open to the world. (Of the five bishoprics of the Byzantine church that eventually developed—Rome, Constantinople, Alexandria, Antioch, and Jerusalem—only Jerusalem was not a seaport.)

By the first century, the common connection between the Jews of the diaspora in the west and those in the east was the Jerusalem temple, until its destruction. The kind of Jews who moved away from Jerusalem westward and settled on and around the Mediterranean

---

8. Stark concludes that it is precisely the features of seaport culture of embracing new and sometimes competing ideas from around the Mediterranean and beyond, along with the constant movement of those ideas through the seaports, that contribute to the early acceptance and rapid spread of Christianity in the large port cities of the Mediterranean. Stark maintains that by the end of the first century, the majority of port cities, sixty-four percent, had a church. In contrast, only twenty-four percent of inland cities had a church at the end of the first century. See Rodney Stark, *Cities of God: The Real Story of How Christianity Became an Urban Movement* (San Francisco: HarperSanFrancisco, 2006), 225–40. While there is some controversy around Stark's data and conclusions, the evidence seems to support Stark's central thesis about the openness and accessibility of port cities that were conducive to the reception of the good news.

Sea tended to be less theologically reactionary compared to those who moved and settled eastward, away from the Mediterranean Sea.[9] While the communities of the eastern diaspora maintained rabbinic connections to Jerusalem, using Hebrew and Aramaic texts like the Mishnah, Midrash, and Talmud and maintaining the rabbinical and oral Jewish traditions, the Jews of the western diaspora became more Hellenized and adopted the Greek language to the extent that Hebrew was replaced, even in synagogue worship, by Greek. The Septuagint (Greek translation of the Hebrew Scriptures) was used by the growing number of Jews who did not speak Hebrew.

With more assimilation to Greek language and culture by the Jews in the west and the preservation of Hebrew language and culture by Jews in the east, the cultural gap between diaspora Jews widened. The Jewish people were becoming in many ways not only the people of the land but increasingly the people of the sea as well, with all of the predictable land/sea tensions observable in history and Scripture.

SAUL OF TARSUS

Saul of Tarsus, the primary actor in the book of Acts and the apostle to the gentiles, was a man of land and sea and as such took advantage of and exacerbated the gap between eastern and western Jews. Paul was the first biblical writer born in a seaport.

> Paul and the early apostles were agents who brokered between two worlds. Paul, a Jew from the Western diaspora (Tarsus in Asia Minor), had one leg in Judea with its Hebrew/Aramaic cultural milieu, but he also traveled to the west and was fluent in Greek. He thus carried in his bag a "religious commodity" from the Land of Israel that he could transmit in Greek—as the rabbis did not and could not.[10]

---

9. A primary source for this summary of the distinctions between the Jewish diaspora of West and East is Doron Mendels, "Why Paul Went West," *Biblical Archaeology Review* 37 (2011): 49–54, 68.

10. Mendels, "Why Paul Went West," 54.

Paul's home city was well connected to the Mediterranean Sea by the Cydnus River. This protected seaport was frequented by powerful and influential people carrying ideas from all over the empire and beyond. Only a generation or two before Paul was born, Pompey, in 67 BC, defeated the pirates who had harassed Tarsus for two decades. Rome took over, making Tarsus the capital of Cilicia, a Roman province. Cicero, Julius Caesar, Mark Anthony, and Cleopatra all spent time in Tarsus. Being born as a Roman citizen, and likely receiving a classical Greek education, Paul was poised for greatness in either the Roman or Jewish world or both. But it was the port of Tarsus that prepared him not only to think like a Greek but also to be "grafted in" to Greek culture.

The apostle Paul was likely not born into a lower social stratum, but following his conversion experience on the road to Damascus, he experienced a spiritual reorientation. He would eventually make a clear decision to utilize the sea as a means of spreading the gospel of Jesus to the rest of the Roman Empire and, in the process, to relate closely to the ritually unclean seafarers and immerse himself in their culture. Arguably, he had a predisposition to doing so because of his origins as a non-Judean Jew and because of the possibility that Pharisees like himself were already engaging in some level of sea travel for religious purposes. Regardless of his predisposition, he could capitalize on the spreading culture of mobility propagated by the Roman government's network of paved roads and protected sea lanes. He utilized not only the physical structures of the empire but also its philosophical and spiritual elements in defining the message of God for both Jews and gentiles connected by the Mediterranean, ultimately ushering in a new understanding of the universality of the kingdom of God.

It was in this reality that the apostle Paul began his missionary journeys, striving to achieve a balance between his Jewish heritage and the pagan world in which he found himself not only a participant but a privileged citizen of Rome. Born and raised within a Hellenized, sea-connected culture, Saul of Tarsus would have encountered anti-sea, land-based reactionaries in his move to Jerusalem for rabbinic study. Thus, both Paul's seaport upbringing and his Pharisaic background and commitments uniquely predisposed him to embrace the life of mission to the gentiles of the Mediterranean. He was a man of two worlds: one liquid and connected, the other land-based and isolated. Some of the ambivalence of the Jerusalem authorities toward Paul stemmed from these cultural contradictions.

Paul, the seafaring, orthodox Jewish representative of Jesus, attempted to establish his authority and influence among everyone in the port cities of the Mediterranean—wealthy elite landowners, sea entrepreneurs, and sea workers—and to unite them into one new social reality. Again, beginning in Acts, and especially with the efforts of Paul, the sea in Scripture becomes the Scripture in the sea.

In light of the kind of people with whom Paul closely associated during his travels with the good news, an estimation of the amount of time Paul spent on ships and in seaports during his mission travels launched from Antioch and ending in Rome is helpful to understand Paul's ability to connect the message of Jesus to both the high-status elites and the sea workers at the bottom of Greek society. How much time did Paul spend around sea workers? My calculations are based on educated guesses of travel times by ship—waiting periods in port cities, times of ministry in port cities, Paul's time in Tarsus prior to studying in Jerusalem, and the time between his conversion and arrival in Antioch at Bartholomew's invitation. The calculations are based only on the travel routes described in Acts. These voyaging records in Acts, while providing remarkably detailed information about the times and distances of Paul's routes, can be verified and even replicated, yet are very likely incomplete.

I conclude that Paul spent about thirty-eight years of his life in seaports and on ships of the Mediterranean, and approximately twenty-two years inland.[11] This includes his imprisonments (Caesarea and

11. For more explanation of the basis of my estimations of Paul's lifetime on land and sea, see the appendix. Part of the difficulty of estimating the length of time of the sea journeys is the contingency of weather, the available space aboard for passengers, and the frequency of the

Rome primarily) and extended ministry in Corinth and Ephesus. What is the significance? Most of Paul's life prior to his study years in Jerusalem as a young man was likely spent in close contact with pagans. Following his return from "Arabia" after the Damascus Road conversion, especially during his years of traveling as recorded in Acts, it is likely that he spent significantly more time with the sea workers at the bottom of the Roman social pyramid than with the elite at the top. It bears repeating: Sea workers were the rough, low-status, often desperate survivors on whom Rome, Paul, and the early Christian movement in the Roman Empire depended.

Estimated lifetime totals

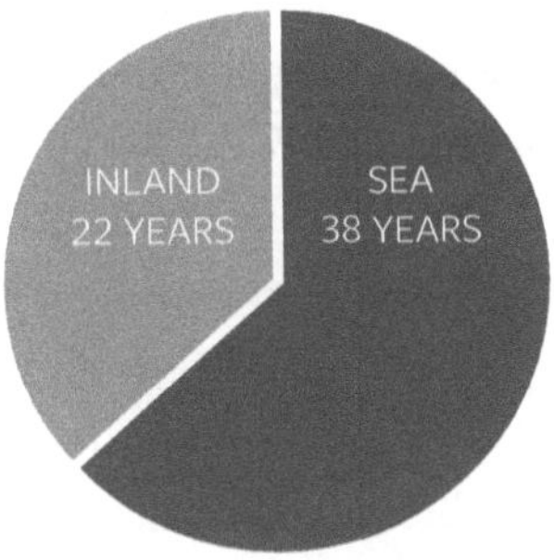

FIGURE 9: **Paul's life on land and sea**

Copyright Linford Stutzman.

Because the passengers and the crew who did the manual labor of sailing aboard both the coastal cargo ships and the larger long-distance vessels shared the same space on deck, there were few secrets.

cargo ships that put into port. "Since no special passenger ships existed in antiquity, travelers had to go to the harbor and ask around until they had found a cargo ship that would travel in their desired direction and take them on board for a charge. ... Sometimes travelers had to wait for weeks or longer until they found a suitable ship. Depending on their destination, they would sometimes have had to carry out their journey in stages, with long waiting periods in between." Catherine Hezser, *Jewish Travel in Antiquity* (Tübingen: Mohr Siebeck, 2011), 182.

Many biblical scholars base their calculations of the times of Paul's sea voyages on ancient texts and simple averages and are not always realistic. Having sailed most of the main routes of Paul in both directions and while keeping a ship's log recording weather conditions, sailing times, and times when sailing was impossible due to too much or not enough wind, and calculating approximate times spent in harbors handling cargo or waiting for the weather to change, I am convinced that most estimations are far too optimistic. I have attempted to factor in the realities of voyaging the Mediterranean solely under sail.

While precise dates of Paul's birth and death are somewhat speculative, the evidence and consensus of the majority of scholars is that Paul was born around 4 BC and was executed under Nero in Rome in around AD 64 or 65. This would make Paul sixty-eight or sixty-nine years old when he died. Considering that my calculations end with Paul in Rome at the end of Acts, with uncertainty about how long he lived before his execution in Rome, my estimates of the amount of time he spent in proximity to sea or inland are still conservative. The proportions of his life are the most important consideration in understanding Paul's context of communicating the gospel, articulating his understanding of Jesus, and instructing those in the churches to which he related how to live.

The conversations, the swearing, the boasting, the crude jokes, the use of "toilets," were all performed in public. Jewish and pagan identities and sensitivities were apparent. Relationships, either positive or negative, were inevitable.

As could be expected, there was often tension aboard the ships of the Mediterranean between those who ran the high-stakes shipping business and those who did the dirty, dangerous, demanding labor of the Roman shipping system—sailing the ships, loading the cargo, producing the equipment, and doing the endless maintenance on the ships needed for Rome's vast shipping system.

SEAPORTS

Seaports such as Antioch, Ephesus, and Corinth were vital links in the Roman shipping system. To appreciate and understand the Christian movement in Acts it is helpful to examine the conditions of the seaports in which Paul founded churches and then attempted to instruct them in his letters. Paul's dramatic encounters with the residents of seaports described in some detail in Athens, Ephesus, and Corinth and the issues that he addresses in his letters to the Christian populations of these primary seaports are best understood within the social dynamics of seaports. There are simmering religious and social tensions among Hellenized seafaring Jews; rabbinic Judean Jews; "God-fearing" pagans; and swaggering, leering sea workers. This was a volatile mix—especially when they all ended up in the same congregation!

Several main seaports and their inhabitants, and the disparate collection of new believers in Jesus who struggled to understand and implement the good news within their thoroughly pagan environment, get most of Luke and Paul's attention in their writings, with good reason. Furthermore, reading Luke's and Paul's writings in the context of seaports and *Mare Nostrum*, with an awareness of the shipping system operated by seafaring exploiters and exploited sea workers, will give Christians living in the West in the twenty-first century a fuller appreciation of and applicable insight into the story with which Christians identify. Christians in the West live in similar conditions.

There are seven key Romanized seaports in the Roman shipping system that are featured in Acts and that likely shaped Paul's attempts throughout his ministry to creatively adapt and develop the message of Jesus in the Mediterranean world. These key seaports are Tarsus, Antioch, Athens, Corinth, Ephesus, Caesarea, and Rome. Except for Athens, Paul spent most of his recorded life in six of these. In four Paul lived and worked voluntarily for extended periods, and in two—Rome and Caesarea—he was a long-term detainee under Rome's judicial system, with Roman soldiers and other prisoners comprising his "focus group" for the good news. All of these seaports were marked by divisions—wealthy and poor; Jews and Greeks; seafaring marginalized and landlubber elite; exploiters and exploited; slaves and free; male dominance and female power; intellectuals and illiterate; huge, world-famous temples and little house churches. Sea travelers participated in the divisions in these seaports and contributed to them. Paul the sea traveler, did as well.

CORINTH

What does a Hebrew Pharisee Roman citizen who believes in a Jew killed by Rome do with a Mediterranean sailor, drunken or otherwise, in the famously debauched city of Corinth? Corinth is not Jerusalem. Corinth is not even Athens, not even close. In the Athens agora, likely in the shade of the stoa, philosophers drew crowds of the idle elite with too much time on their hands looking for an interesting idea from a Jewish stranger they could argue about later. A traveler to Corinth would be more likely than in any other Mediterranean port to encounter drunken brawls; outrageous behavior; elaborate and bawdy entertainment; the swaggering, noisy sea workers returning down from their worship of Aphrodite at the famous temple above the town; and the boisterous crowds, sometimes angry, sometimes debauched, always unpredictable. An upright, respectable traveler coming to Corinth for the first time, pagan or Jew, might be scandalized and leave as soon as possible. Paul came and stayed, for Paul from Tarsus was at home everywhere—Jerusalem, Athens, and Corinth. Paul was neither your average Roman citizen nor a Pharisee concerned about being contaminated. He was a cross-cultural adapter of the news about Jesus of Nazareth.

But while Paul could quickly get a hearing and gain some respect in Athens on the basis of his brilliant philosophical rhetoric, those same rhetorical skills, he likely discovered quickly, would get him targeted as the butt of ribald jokes, crude mocking, hilarious mimicking. How does an educated Roman citizen win the respect of sailors? What did Paul say to a crowd of rough, raunchy sailors in Corinth, drunken or sober, who were desperate enough for some respect, status, justice, stability, and love that they were attracted to Paul's message of Jesus?

Paul focused his ministry where his influence was so effective that it generated both large numbers of enthusiastic followers and large, angry mobs. I suspect that Paul, in port cities like Corinth and Ephesus, liked to think of Jesus in Jerusalem as his standard for how to have an effective impact on the crowds.

The dramatic positive and negative encounters in Corinth, vividly described in Acts 18, and then in Ephesus, in Acts 19, along with his letters to the astonishingly pagan Christians in Corinth, were the basis, I believe, of Paul's "boasting" in his second letter to the Corinthians. "Boasting" is actually what Paul calls it, one of the ways he has "become all things to all people" (1 Cor 9:22). He is establishing his credentials in the way that the low-class sea workers of the Mediterranean do.

"Paul boasts about his sufferings" is how most commentaries label that most unusual text in 2 Corinthians 11:16–33. Yes, it is a recital of suffering, maybe even with lines borrowed from the ribald, rebellious yarns sailors and port workers told each other or sang together in tavernas. But as with all this kind of sailor-talk, the point is not about the suffering as much as the survival of suffering, the triumph over those who inflicted the pain. To not only survive but to thumb your nose at authority would provide the credentials you needed to win respect among your sailor/sea-worker peers in Corinth. Fancy

FIGURE 10: **Temple of Apollo in ancient Corinth**

rhetoric would not do it. Sailors would understand the kind of suffering Paul talks about because they have suffered in the same way.

Look at this bragging. There is nothing quite like it in the Hebrew or Greek Scriptures from any hero of faith. Most of the things Paul brags about are a shame to either elite pagans, religious Jews, or both. This list will only win credibility among people who themselves have experienced similar mistreatment, abuse, and injustice under Roman power. It is the antiauthority-based authority of underclass self-organization, like that of the criminal mob or street gangs today who exist in a system of exploitation or huge status imbalance. To survive, the sea workers needed to cooperate with the Roman economic system that exploited them, but any opportunity to defy that system successfully earned credibility, status, and leadership roles within the sea-worker "mob."

Paul defied political authority before and after his conversion. And he talked about it. His zealous persecution of the believers in Damascus was not exactly sanctioned by Rome. Paul's daring, creative escape from being arrested by the officials of the Nabatean King Aretas in Damascus would get applause from runaway slaves, wanted criminals, and other various rebels.

"To the Jews, I became as a Jew," Paul writes to the Corinthians (1 Cor 9:20). And then he both brags and demonstrates this when he cites his Pharisee credentials, catalogs his adherence to the Law, circumcises the pagan/Jewish Timothy in Lystra, and makes public vows to impress the Jerusalem Jewish community. Paul the Jewish zealot never seems to be especially successful in establishing his Jewish credentials among his fellow Jews who do not accept his message of Jesus.

"I became as a Greek" appears to have worked better for Paul. Maybe. Because in Corinth, his authority to intervene in the lives of those believers who considered themselves free to "sin boldly" was put to the test. Yet while it is not clear how effective Paul's boasting was in exercising authority in that fledgling church in which the elite and the underclass ate, prayed, and quarreled together in the luxurious and sordid port of Corinth, the church that Paul started in Corinth exists to this day.

According to the chronology of Acts, Paul spends a total of up to four years in the two most connected and powerful seaports on the trade routes between Rome and the eastern parts of the Mediterranean. That would be about one-third of his time of recorded mission activity. At the end of his last mission journey, returning to Jerusalem, he leaves Corinth and then sails by Ephesus to Miletus, another famous seaport, where he meets with the leaders of the Ephesian church.[12]

12. The story in Acts states that Paul did not want to be delayed as he wanted to make it back to Jerusalem in time for Pentecost (Acts 20:16). The potential for delay because of stopping in Ephesus was likely. There may have been other, unstated reasons for avoiding Ephesus. I believe it is likely that the coastal freighter Paul had been on since Assos was originally headed for Miletus, and this would be the ship Paul took because it was directly on the route east, saving time. Paul could easily continue on that ship or catch another one heading eastward.

CONCLUSIONS

Sea workers carried the gospel. Like modern viruses, the stealth and uncontrollable spread from seaport to seaport occurred via the yarn-spinning sea workers. Whether or not these sea workers believed in the message of Paul and his fellow travelers who spent so much time aboard, sea workers were in the position to share the rumors of the kingdom. Not only were the sea workers constantly moving, but the subculture of sea workers that included both connection and rootlessness, as well as antiauthoritarian impulses and rebellion, may have contributed as much as or more than the basic openness of seaport populations or the *Pax Romana* that is often cited as the ideal time for the spread of the gospel.[13]

Sea workers were part of the Christian communities in the port cities. These churches contained land-holding elites, sea entrepreneurs, and sea workers. This is especially visible in Corinth, where the social tensions of Mediterranean seaports are famously exhibited. Problems in the seaport of Corinth are indicative of the social composition and related tensions in the church in Corinth, as well as churches in other seaports.

Paul possessed and further developed the skills to win the respect of sea workers. Paul's letters contain evidence of his skill at earning his authority among sea workers in the port city churches, at Corinth especially. This is especially clear in 2 Corinthians 11:24–26, in which Paul sounds like a non-Jewish seaman. Like Jesus speaking the language of Galilean fishermen, Paul spoke the language of sea workers in the Mediterranean. In addition to their shared approach to communication, Jesus and Paul both identified closely with the marginalized. Their message both connected with and challenged the

13. The debate on how the Christian message spread so quickly in the Mediterranean Roman world is lively. Currently a similar debate about how "conspiracy theories" spread so quickly along educational and social class lines is perhaps helpful. Is it the communications systems of the internet and social media platforms, or the exploitation of the systems and platforms by the disenfranchised, greedy, exploiters, dividers, and others, including those who tell the truth, promote unity, and share any kind of authentically good news with others?

antiestablishment assumptions of the marginalized, for Paul, like Jesus, recognized that the marginalized, with their antiauthoritarian bent, had great potential, qualities, and value. Like Paul, they were not easily intimidated.

Paul, like Jesus, sought to relate the gospel to everyone. From the marginalized sea workers on the bottom to the wealthy and powerful of the Roman system, from slaves to the religious Jewish leaders of diaspora synagogues—Paul's words and actions are of radical inclusion rather than incitement to joining one group with (legitimate) grievances against another. He was all things to all sea workers, as well as to the land elite. This was a high-risk endeavor, filled with the hazard of disappointing one side or another, or everyone. But Paul, like Jesus and the sea workers of the Mediterranean, was a risk taker, willing to boast in the social stigma of sea-worker credentials. The Greek New Testament, and especially the writings of Luke and Paul, who spent so much of their lives in seaports, is shaped by the sea and its people.

The hazards for Paul, as for Jesus before and for the Christian movement in the Mediterranean following, emanated from both Rome and Jerusalem. As growing numbers of the marginalized from the ends of the earth joined the movement of the good news of Jesus that was traveling by sea, the alarm of those responsible for maintaining Rome's agenda in the seaports of the Mediterranean grew as well. The story of the sea and its people in Scripture will culminate on a small island in the Aegean.

REFLECTIONS FROM THE SEA

The opportunities and potential for bright, curious young boys like Paul, growing up in a seaport on the Mediterranean, are still clear. We were overlooking the ancient harbor of Antalya, from where Barnabas and Paul had left at the end of their first mission journey to return to Antioch. I was lecturing to a group of students about how growing up in a Hellenistic seaport would likely have given the young Saul exposure to the Greeks and perhaps some admiration of their ideas and culture.

I noticed a Turkish boy who looked to be about twelve years old eagerly crowd in close to listen about the advantages Saul had growing up in Tarsus rather than in Jerusalem. The boy stayed for the entire lecture. After I finished, he wanted to talk to me more about Saul and his later exploits as the apostle Paul, someone he had never heard about. I was happy for the conversation, appreciating his curiosity and marveling at his English-speaking skills. At the end, I asked him why he had been listening in. He replied, "I love to hear ideas from visitors from different countries. I love talking to people from all over the world about their ideas. I am trying to learn as many languages as I can so I can go anywhere in the world one day. I am really glad I live in Antalya. If I lived anywhere else in Turkey I wouldn't get this chance."

I realized that I had talked with the twelve-year-old Saul in Tarsus.

REFLECTIONS FROM THE SEA

I had admired Paul long before going to sea with him. But on the day Janet and I untied for our first time the stiff ropes of *SailingActs* in Volos, Greece, to begin the voyage, I got to know Paul in a new way.

For about the first thirty minutes, as the waving spectators on the wharf shrank from view, Janet and I were overwhelmed with emotions running from elation to terror. The elation ended in minute thirty-one, when we suddenly observed huge, black clouds directly behind us, with a curtain of rain so intense the landscape we had just left completely disappeared. We just stared as it moved closer, and the wind picked up. Then everything hit at once, huge gusts of wind, thunder, lightning, torrential rain, chaos. Janet scampered below, closing the gangway on the way down into the cabin. I pulled my new foul weather gear (which I would use on only one other occasion in the next twenty years) over my soaked clothes. This was not a good beginning.

A Greek yacht whisked by us, the captain nonchalantly giving a little wave, shaking his head ever so slightly. Pity. Seafarer and landlubber.

Then the squall ended. The following day, after we recovered somewhat at an overnight anchorage, we attempted, under the appreciative gaze of a gaggle of onlookers on the dock on the first island we came to, our first attempt at the dreaded "Mediterranean mooring."[14] It took perhaps ten attempts before we succeeded, without collision, in tying up next to the boat of the Greek sailor who had waved as he passed us in the squall two days earlier. He and the other amused onlookers on the dock watched the whole time.

"Could I come on your boat," the Greek sailor asked, "and explain a few things to you?"

For the next forty-five minutes on board *SailingActs,* the seasoned Greek sailor patiently explained tactics for dealing with the vagaries of the Mediterranean, for making improvements on trimming the sails, and most importantly, for exactly how to do a Mediterranean mooring in a crowded marina.

The Greek seafarer, in sharing his care and wisdom, helped me understand how Paul became "as a Greek" by admiring and learning from their wisdom while reflecting on the gospel of Jesus.

---

14. Zeke Quezada, "Mediterranean Mooring: What Is It and Why?" American Association of Sailing, https://asa.com/news/2023/01/10/mediterranean-mooring-what-is-it-and-why/. "The Mediterranean Moor is a hybrid of anchoring, rafting, and docking used in regions where there is little room and tidal range. It takes its name from an old Mediterranean custom of mooring stern-to along a town's quay or sea wall and it allows a lot of boats to fit in a small place. In principle, you drop an anchor in the middle of the harbor and tie the stern to the quay, but the execution takes knowledge of how your boat behaves in reverse and skill in getting lines ashore." Quezada adds: "All of this is easier said than done. Sailboats with extensive prop walk will wreak havoc on your plan to simply back up. Crosswinds will give you white knuckles and tight, busy marinas will drive you mad. The benefit of walking off your boat to a crowd of admirers will make it all worth it."

CHAPTER 6

NAVIGATION: THE SEA CHANGE IN SCRIPTURE

"Then I saw a new heaven and a new earth;
for the first heaven and the first earth had passed away,
and the sea was no more."
Revelation 21:1

FROM ROME TO PATMOS

The story of the Mediterranean Sea in Acts ends in Rome. Connected to the Mediterranean Sea by the Tiber River and thus to every other seaport around its rim, and every major seaport and tiny anchorage of every island in the sea, Rome rules the sea. The seaports are connected by excellent roads to all of the inland cities of the empire. It rules the land. Rome rules the entire Mediterranean world. Caesar is lord. Hail, king of the Egyptians, Philistines, Phoenicians, Greeks, Italians, and Judeans/Palestinians.

It is within this reality that the New Testament was written. From the good divisions between sea, sky, and land by the Creator and Sustainer of all things; through the story of God's promise to Abraham of the Land and his descendants' encountering God's power over the Red Sea; through the ongoing encounter with the people of the Mediterranean Sea, their enemies, and their occupiers, the perception of the sea—positive, negative, or neutral—depends on whether God or humans are in control.

Jesus on the Sea of Galilee is in control. The early seafaring Christians were fearlessly proclaiming the good news of the coming kingdom under the authority and power of God, who is in control. But Rome still ruled, evil existed, and the threat of enemies to the tiny movement of Christians on and around the sea remained. The final reference to the sea before Revelation opens is metaphorical, depicting evil people who, like the sea, are out of control. They are described as like the "wild waves of the sea, casting up the foam of their own shame" (Jude 1:13). So while the story of the people of the Land responding to the sea and its people from the beginning of Scripture to the end is not consistently either positive or negative, promising or perilous, while there is some growing accommodation to the reality of the sea in terms of Jewish trade, travel, and political alliances, it is always done at the risk of loss—of identity, of fidelity to God, of holiness. The division between the people of the land and the people of the sea and the threat they presented is a theme chronicled throughout the entire Hebrew Scripture. With the Greek and then the Roman invaders, the triumph of the seaborne masters of the sea was complete. Any challenge to Rome's dominion, real or imagined, would be costly.

EPHESUS

The final act of the drama of the sea in Scripture begins in the mighty seaport of Ephesus. It is for very good reasons that Paul and other leaders had spent so much time in Ephesus. David deSilva notes, "Few cities in the Mediterranean were more important in the story of the emerging church than Ephesus."[1] Ephesus was a leading seaport

1. David A. deSilva, "The Social and Geographical World of Ephesus," in *Lexham Geographic Commentary on Acts through Revelation*, ed. Barry J. Beitzel (Bellingham, WA: Lexham Press, 2019), 537–53. See deSilva's description of Ephesus, its status in the empire, and the lengthy and effective ministry of Paul in Ephesus.

with perhaps two hundred thousand residents, making it one of the largest cities in the empire.[2]

The renowned Temple of Artemis, one of the popular tourist destinations and pilgrimage sites, with associated businesses, made Ephesus a primary seaport connecting the southern Aegean to Corinth and Rome. Connected by roads across Asia Minor, Ephesus was a strategic center from where the gospel spread (Acts 19:10). Sometime after Paul had left Ephesus after the riot of silversmiths worried about losing their image business, John arrived.[3]

The church at Ephesus, under the leadership of John, grew to the point that John was deemed a threat to the authorities and exiled to Patmos. From the thriving church in Ephesus, additional churches were beginning to grow to the extent that the authorities of these wealthy trade centers were becoming concerned. John was considered to pose some kind of threat to the status quo and was removed to Patmos. This exile was likely the decision of the provincial governor, a sentence of banishment for a limited time.[4]

ISLANDS

The final view of the sea and its people in Scripture is from the perspective of a seemingly insignificant island. Patmos is a small island of the Aegean (the northernmost island of the Dodecanese) lying about thirty miles (48 km) off the coast of Asia Minor (present-day Turkey). Patmos provided the two necessary functions of Rome: security and social control. It provided a navy presence close enough to

---

2. Jerome Murphy-O'Connor, *St. Paul's Ephesus: Texts and Archaeology* (Collegeville, MN: Liturgical Press, 2008), 131–32.

3. Hard evidence that the apostle John ministered in Ephesus and was banished to Patmos from there does not exist. Early and later church tradition, the association of John's Epistles with the recipients from Ephesus and its environs, and the circumstantial evidence of history form the basis of a broad consensus among scholars that John spent significant time in Ephesus. The banishment to the nearby island of Patmos adds some geographical credibility.

4. Mark Wilson, "Geography of the Island of Patmos," in Beitzel, *Lexham Geographic Commentary on Acts through Revelation*, 624. For an extensive description of Patmos and its significance in Rome's control of the seaports, shipping routes, and the inhabitants in those seaports, see pages 619–28.

the shipping routes and primary ports to protect them. And Patmos also was ideal for exile, for it was isolated enough that people whom Rome banished to the island were effectively silenced.

Patmos, as were many other Aegean islands, was an ideal place for Rome to protect its commercial and political interests. A mere day or two's sail from Ephesus, Patmos was close enough for easy deportation and far enough from the nearest island or mainland to be secure. Patmos is not directly on the route of the main shipping lane along the western coast of Asia Minor but is close enough to protect that route and the great seaport of Miletus that lies to its southeast on the mainland. Patmos is large enough to house a harbor that could accommodate a sizable navy fleet. It is also large enough to support a small population of perhaps up to three thousand people, including exiled "guests," and small enough to keep an eye on every vessel.

Rome's utilization of islands for its domination of the Mediterranean, discussed earlier, gives perspective on John's exile on Patmos. It was a part of Rome's efforts to control the restive inhabitants of the empire by limiting or facilitating the activities of people who served its purposes, who lived on the rim of the sea and sailed the routes between ports. Patmos exemplifies how Rome dominated the Mediterranean by controlling the connections, the ports, and the cities connected directly to them. It controlled and utilized the islands to protect the shipping lanes and the seaports and, in the case of Patmos and many other similar islands, to isolate rebels. Islands are both isolated and connected.

The connections, due to the time, effort, and risk required of anyone who makes the voyage, are "purposeful" connections for trade, security, and control. This makes them distinct from mainland seaports. Mainland seaports are the most connected cities of an empire, but getting to them requires less intentionality and resolve than island seaports, as all travelers and cargo headed toward Rome passed through the major seaport cities.

In contrast to *all* roads leading to Rome, *no* roads lead to island seaports. Travelers who had a choice needed good reasons and

FIGURE 11: **Sailing to Patmos from the east**

motivation to make the voyage to the islands. In the Roman maritime system, trade and security were the two primary reasons for sailing to islands. The small islands, in and alongside the coastal shipping lanes and just off the mainland of Asia Minor and Greece, could be used as fortified naval bases, monitoring and securing the marine traffic from the vantage point of limited accessibility that could be easily monitored. Islands were a vital part of Rome's system of domination.

Patmos is isolated, and its connections are very specific.[5] Under Roman control, the sea connections with Patmos were less for trade

5. "Islands are a connecting point between land and sea, and can be regarded as a station on the route of a sea passage." For a fascinating summary of the study of the distinctive sociocultural character of islands, see Guoqing Ma, "Islands and the World from an Anthropological Perspective," *International Journal of Anthropology and Ethnology* 4 (2020), https://doi.org/10.1186/s41257-020-00038-x. I conducted several informal interviews with people on Patmos asking this question: "Do you feel isolated or connected living on Patmos?" All of the answers were invariably the same. "Both." "Why?" I asked. A typical reply ran, "Because the only people who come to Patmos have a reason to visit. Maybe to come as a pilgrim, maybe to learn more about Patmos, sometimes for business. When we go to the mainland or other big islands, we go for some good reason too. But we can come back any time and get away from the things we

and more for security than the major islands like Samos, Kos, Chios, Rhodes, and Cyprus. These larger islands on the shipping routes had far more purposeful trade connections than the smaller islands like Patmos on the margins.

Except for Cyprus, Paul did not voluntarily spend much time on islands on the shipping routes, and he spent no time at all on the small islands off the shipping routes, choosing the large mainland seaports for his residential ministry. Mainland seaports are exposed to everyone, in contrast to islands, which are more like oases in deserts, isolated but with purposeful connections. Islands were useful for the Roman Empire for controlling its population and less useful for the emissaries of the kingdom of God for connecting the good news with a restive population.

So Paul may have recognized that the purposeful-but-limited connectivity of islands was less conducive than the seaports to the spread of the gospel. The coastal seaports are the places where radically different kinds of inhabitants and travelers interact constantly. Ideas circulate freely. Islands have a culture that is shaped by both their isolation and their connectivity simultaneously. Islands are mini cultures constantly interacting with mainland culture while maintaining distinctiveness. Paul's longest stay on any island after Cyprus, the first island at the beginning of his first missionary voyage, is probably Malta, the last island on his journey to Rome. Paul was on Malta not by choice but by accident. He was a prisoner along with the other shipwreck survivors and would be rescued, also as a prisoner, by Rome.[6]

---

don't like about the problems that other places have when there are too many people who do not know each other, living very close together."

6. Malta is one of the most Christian not only of all the islands of the Mediterranean but of all countries in the world—98.1 percent. Saint Paul is their patron saint. Of the top ten countries with the highest percentage of Christians in the world, eight are islands. Interviewing islanders on islands visited by Paul in the Acts story, I was impressed that the pride and the positive memory of Paul's visit to their island, no matter how short the visit was, were clearly greater than those of people I interviewed in the mainland seaports. It appears that islanders, especially those living on islands that are somewhat remote, value the risk-taking, intentional

JOHN

The writer of Revelation, John, was an effective, influential leader.[7] Rome's cruel punishment of popular leaders, such as Jesus, by crucifixion did not always halt the momentum of the message. Punishment of popular leaders of any kind, especially cruel punishment of nonviolent crimes, was difficult to justify. So it is likely that John, who, from the point of view of the provincial authorities, might indeed have been involved in a destabilizing movement based on a dubious conspiracy, needed to be silenced—but without making him a martyr, which could exacerbate the problem. The islands of *Mare Nostrum* were ideal for silencing troublemakers by isolation.

John was sentenced to a limited period of exile and likely taken directly to Patmos from Ephesus. The sea on which the good news was carried westward toward the end of the earth as promised by Jesus had become for John the end of his ability to communicate with his churches or to carry that message farther. It would be the farthest west he would sail.

It hardly matters whether John the writer of Revelation is the same John the fisherman on the Sea of Galilee or another John, who knew little of the sea. It is clear that the writer shares a rather typical Jewish ambivalence toward the Mediterranean Sea. For anyone banished to an island in the Mediterranean under complete control of the Roman navy, the sea is the context of evil.

John the writer of Revelation, cut off from the flourishing churches he helped establish and lead on the mainland, mentions "the sea"

---

voyager more than the inhabitants of mainland seaports, who experience a steady stream of important visitors, do.

7. The identity of John the author of Revelation is an ongoing dispute, as there are many traditions. Dating is also disputed. Many scholars date Revelation toward the end of the first century. An alternative is to date Revelation during the reign of Nero (AD 54–68) and before the destruction of Jerusalem in AD 70. Mark Wilson argues that the John of Revelation is John the Evangelist and that the evidence supports the dating of Revelation in about AD 69, just before the destruction of Jerusalem. See Mark Wilson, *Victory through the Lamb: A Guide to Revelation in Plain Language* (Wooster, OH: Weaver, 2014), 28–29. I believe that the early traditions of the church on the identity of John and the early dating are just as credible, if not more so, than the alternatives of two or three "Johns" and a late first-century dating of Revelation.

more than any other writer of Greek Scripture.[8] The island might be John's place of exile, but it is the sea that prevents his communication or escape back to the mainland. He can see the mainland, but he cannot leave the island until the authorities deem him old enough to no longer be a threat to their domination.

What does that tell us about John on Patmos? He is isolated. He is disconnected from his people. He is alone. He has gone from the hyperconnected seaport of Ephesus to the connected-but-isolated island of Patmos. The description of the sea in Revelation is especially negative, representing the Roman system of sea-based evil controlling the economy, politics, loyalties, and hearts and minds through seduction and violence.[9]

REVELATION

Revelation has the last word in Scripture. Following the opening introduction (Rev 1:1–8), the beginning words from John about himself (Rev 1:9) in the concluding sea-surrounded book of the New Testament, likely written last, parallel the first words of Hebrew Scripture. The context of John's isolation, like the waters before the first act of creation, is "without form and void." Only in this case, the power of Rome is "on the face of the deep." The moving wind is not the wind of God.

Then, unexpectedly, the living, triumphant King of kings, Jesus, suddenly appears to John on Patmos. Hearing the "loud voice like a trumpet," John turns. He is so startled and terrified by the power and

8. "Sea" is used twenty-four times, likely referring to the Mediterranean Sea, either literally or metaphorically.

9. The enormous effort and resources required to maintain control of the seas began to decline in the centuries following the first-century high point of Roman control among the people living around the Mediterranean Sea. The positive Greek attitude, along with that of the early Christian attitude toward the sea, gradually became more negative. There are likely many factors for this growing negativity. For Rome, the effort and expense of maintaining control eventually became unsustainable. Did John's experience on Patmos and the book of Revelation contribute to the growing negativity of the early church toward the sea in the following centuries?

glory of the "Son of Man" that he falls as though dead to the ground. "Do not be afraid!" says the Creator (Rev 1:10–17).

While attempting to decipher the precise meaning of the vivid pictures painted in Revelation has kept biblical scholars and self-proclaimed prophets busy for almost two millennia, the central and most important message for believers and followers of Jesus is the first four words of Jesus. Jesus explains why John and the readers of the book do not need to live in fear. The remainder of Revelation is a graphic presentation of the terrifying power struggles of history and the future, culminating in the triumph of Jesus over death itself.

"Do not be afraid" was the implied message to the disciples on the Mount of Olives when he commissioned them to witness to the ends of the earth by land and sea (Acts 1:8). The promised power at Pentecost that launched the Christian movement had taken the apostles and others as far as they could travel. It had taken Paul, John, and many others throughout the Mediterranean world by land and sea to the extent that Rome was increasingly concerned at the revolutionary popularity of the Christian movement. The message from Pentecost to Patmos to the ends of the earth that has enabled the Christian movement for two thousand years is "do not be afraid."

But John is still on Patmos, surrounded by a sea that Rome controls. The view of the "the deep" from Patmos is a reservoir of evil powers, some hidden, some on public display. So you can hear John's joy when he declares "the sea was no more" in the new heaven and new earth in the new creation of the future (Rev 21:1). This is the last time the sea is mentioned in Scripture. The first time is in the story of creation.

As a sailor who respects and even loves the Mediterranean Sea with all of its instability, unpredictability, chaos, and threat, I find the omission of the sea from the vision of the new heaven and new earth to be troubling. Is John really envisioning that seventy percent of the old earth is going to be replaced by solid, fertile ground, along with sand, rocks, and dust only? Is the new creation devoid of the delight of a broad reach on a sparkling blue sea or the joy that comes in the dazzling beauty of another Mediterranean sunrise, the "rosy-fingered dawn" warming the waters of the sea and the hearts of the seafarers? Is there to be, in the new creation, the bliss of a gentle anchorage with the gentle lullaby of tinkling goat bells, chirping crickets, and tiny splashes of the little waves as the sinking sun paints the sea, sky, and landscape with shades of purples and pinks?

Is it the *mare* that is to be no more, or is it *Mare Nostrum*—the domination of the Mediterranean in which Rome can isolate John from his churches? Is the sea that is being destroyed referring to the control of Rome over the sea? The control that eliminates the opportunity for anyone who does not give allegiance to the "divine" Caesar to either buy or sell anything? A system of sea-based trade that utterly dominates the economic system in a way that enslaves and exploits many whose livelihoods are connected to and by the sea, and lavishly and wastefully rewards the rulers of that same sea?

I believe the answer to all of these questions is "no." I believe that John is describing the new creation of heaven and earth as fulfilling the intent of the original creation. In this one, as in the beginning, the sea is there, part of the creation that God defined at the end of the third day and specifically pronounced as "good."

At least that is what I hope John is describing: the end of *Mare Nostrum*—our sea—and the beginning of *Mare Domini*—our Lord's sea. This sea no longer represents chaos because of the new creation. The sea no longer divides but rather unites all creation. I like to imagine that the sailors of the Mediterranean, transferring John to or from Patmos, had heard John talk about Jesus, the living Lord of lords, the Lord of land and sea, who would one day liberate the sea and even sailors from the domination of Rome. I like to think they remembered him and the promise of the kingdom of God and that they, as typical sailors, told that story to others in seaports.

SUMMARY

Division: From creation to new creation, Scripture, history, and cultures are shaped by the divisions of land and sea and its peoples. Hebrew Scripture chronicles the divisions.

Perils: Hebrew Scripture is about the perils of the sea and its people, as well as the power of God to deliver his people from the sea and its people.

Domination: Hebrew Scripture is also about the people of the sea who adapt to its challenges and amass power and wealth by controlling the people living around the rim of the Mediterranean, including the people of the Promised Land. Beginning with the Hebrews' confrontation of the Philistines in the Land, the story ends in Greek Scripture with Roman domination of *Mare Nostrum*.

Potential: The rewards of developing positive relationships with Phoenicians, Greeks, and Romans, as well as the disadvantages of noncooperation, form the context of much of Hebrew Scripture to the very end of Greek Scripture. The economic, political, and social advantages attract some in the Land and repel others, dividing kings and prophets, faithful and less faithful, rich and poor. Land and sea divisions underly the divisions among the people of the Land in Scripture.

Competition: The story of Jesus is a revolutionary shift in the narrative from land to sea. While Judea is under Roman occupation, the kingdom of God embodied, demonstrated, and explained by Jesus is present throughout the region of Galilee, including around the Sea of Galilee, traveling by fishing boats and fishermen. The gospel of the kingdom begins to be so attractive, especially to those who had suffered economically, spiritually, and physically, that Rome and its self-interested cooperators crucify Jesus. Acts and the remainder of the Greek Scriptures tell the story of the triumph, once again, of the power of God, who is in control of land and sea, life and death.

Navigation: Acts and the remainder of Greek Scriptures are also about, to, and by people who have accepted and carried the good news of the kingdom of God on land and sea. Not only is the Scripture in the sea, but it has also become the Scripture of the sea's people. The good news of the kingdom has been carried by the sea to the ends of the earth.

The story of the sea in Scripture ends looking triumphantly ahead to when, if divisions exist, they will again be "good."

Conclusion

NAVIGATING THE SEA AFTER SCRIPTURE

The story of the sea in history continues. In subsequent centuries the sea's people continued to sail the Mediterranean, which was still dominated by Rome. While the Christian movement began as a kind of subversive, popular, seaborne movement that ended in Scripture on the island of Patmos, the Mediterranean Sea was still controlled by Rome.

With Emperor Constantine and the Edict of Milan, *Mare Nostrum* begins to take on a new meaning. Constantinople begins to function as the new Rome, now a thalassocracy of the kingdom of God! But, as history attests, it is not a peaceable kingdom. For although the Mediterranean has been repurposed, it is not necessarily under the control of the Spirit of Jesus.

In the Mediterranean of history, violence and barbarity, now in the name of God, continue under Byzantine, Crusader, and Muslim invaders. The battles by empires, Christian or not—it does not seem to make much difference—continue, out of the Strait of Gibraltar, across the Atlantic to the New World. The kingdom of God, once transported by cargo ships in the Roman system, is now carried by warships. Seaborne promises of globalization along with the perils of war, pollution, enslavement in new forms, refugees, and suffering continue to this day to the ends of the earth.

The world in which we live has not only been shaped by the sea; it has become increasingly like the sea.

The seafaring followers of Jesus in the first century were like the sea and its people, especially the seafarers, flexible and fearless at the same time, for they knew that Jesus was Lord of land and sea and would win over all powers of evil on land and sea. God brought his people through the wilderness of land and would bring them across the wildness of the sea. Jesus brought his followers on land and sea safely this far, and he will lead us home. Like the seafaring followers of Jesus on the Sea of Galilee, we too must fearlessly go down again to wider seas.

Paul's readiness and ability to identify with everyone in the most flamboyantly debauched and violent port cities of the Mediterranean and his high-risk attempt to establish his credibility among everyone from the bottom to the top of society are extremely relevant for Christians, especially in the West. Like Paul the Roman citizen, we live in a globally united and painfully divided world. Our world at the beginning of the twenty-first century increasingly resembles the Roman Mediterranean Sea in the first century. The gospel, spread by the movement of sea workers with Paul the land traveler and seafarer, offers possibilities for the church in times of unprecedented movement, change, and instability on a global scale. We must fearlessly go down to the sea again like Paul and the early seafaring Christians, following Jesus.

We, like the early seafaring Christians, those fearless pilgrims of hope, also continue this voyage of faith and life in similar conditions, for the world is like the sea.

THE WORLD IS LIKE THE SEA

Like the Mediterranean Sea, our world as always is unpredictable, unstable, changeable, and simultaneously beautiful and deadly. Like the sea, our world is full of potential and peril, so promising and so disappointing. We are connected globally as never before in history by communication, information, and trade as if everyone now lives around the Mediterranean Sea. The natural and cultural storms at sea affect all of us everywhere.[1]

As in the days of Rome's commerce and control, the natural and cultural seas are deeply divided by superpowers vying for dominance and various rebel groups resisting it. This sea-like world is, as always, simultaneously threatening and promising. This is what John sees on Patmos, surrounded by the waters, before and after his vision.

"*E pluribus unum*" is a product of the Roman infrastructure on land and the domination of the Mediterranean Sea for the first and last time in history. But John sees beyond Patmos and the waters to the time when the sea-like world in which he is living is no more, when all of humanity, from every tribe, tongue, and nation, is gathered around the throne of God, and "*e pluribus unum*" is finally a reality.

But in the meantime, John's vision from Patmos informs the Christian church that is surrounded by the seas that appear to be in trouble and rising. Communities living in settlements next to the sea make decisions on how to respond to the rising sea levels due to global warming. The Christian church, threatened by the rising seas of culture, also has necessary choices to make to protect its faith communities. Cultural inundation; the erosion of the once solid theological cliffs on which beautiful religious edifices are built; and the threat of incoming tides sweeping away cherished beliefs and practices, and even our children, are all existential threats. What are the choices? Ignore or deny? Move to higher ground? Build dikes? All of the conditions above were experienced by the Jews of Judea under Roman occupation. The various Jewish parties made the choices of the responses above. Jesus and

1. "Six out of ten inhabitants of the 'blue planet' now live on or within 100 kilometers of the seashore." Don Hinrichsen, *Our Common Seas: Coasts in Crisis* (London: Routledge, 1990), 1. This study of the destruction of all seas on the planet makes the case that most of the world's population chooses to live on or near the coasts and uses the sea as a kind of self-cleansing garbage dump. All kinds of human pollution occur on every coast of the world, affecting the entire planet. While descriptive of the global environment, it is also metaphorical. The cultural and moral pollution of our sea-like connected world is global.

his followers did not. All of the seaport churches of the Mediterranean in the first century faced all of the conditions above. Paul's actions demonstrated the choices of Jesus and his followers, and his letters to these seaport churches directed them to do likewise.

Jesus, inviting his disciples aboard boats for the non-Jewish shores around the Sea of Galilee, or the apostles after Pentecost moving westward to the seashore, then on around the entire rim of the Mediterranean, went fearlessly to sea to the ends of the earth. Jesus invites us, his representatives, to do the same.

THE CHURCH IS LIKE A SHIP AT SEA

A depiction of the church used very frequently by early Christians around the Mediterranean was a ship at sea.[2] Noah's ark as a symbol of salvation, the boat stories of Jesus on the Sea of Galilee taking his disciples toward ministry and through storms, the book of Acts, and the familiarity of the sea and voyaging to the seaport churches give the ship image biblical and experiential relevance.

A ship on a successful voyage is at home on the untamed sea while not being overcome, overwhelmed, or controlled by it. The church is on a promising, high-risk voyage toward the vision of the kingdom of God, inviting everyone aboard. This ship-church as always is at home in its culture but not controlled by it. The motley collection of humanity attracted to a healthy Christian community is like passengers aboard ships, united in commitment despite the risks, cooperating to reach a common goal, and utilizing the power of both the

2. "Another early and accepted emblem of the Church was the ship. In the Apostolic Constitutions (II, xlvii) the bishop surrounded by the assembly of the faithful is compared to the helmsman of a ship; but the idea is as old as Tertullian (De bap., xii; P. L., l, 1214) and it was varied sometimes by comparing the Church to the ark of Noah. In any case the ship was a recognized Christian symbol and Clement of Alexandria approved it for a signet ring. 'Let the dove or the fish,' he says, 'the vessel flying before the wind,—or the marine anchor be our signets' (Paed. III, ii; P. G., VIII, 633), and numerous representations of ships, sometimes serving as the design for a lamp, with the figure of Christ or St. Peter as helmsman are preserved to us. The name which we still retain for the 'nave' (French, *nef*) of a church bears testimony to the persistence of the same idea." Herbert Thurston, "Symbolism," in *The Catholic Encyclopedia*, vol. 14 (New York: Robert Appleton Company, 1912), 375.

untamed winds of the Spirit and the powerful, prevailing winds of culture to make progress by constantly adjusting the sails and the ship's heading. As with ancient sailing ships, progress toward the destination is not in a straight line.

Like the ship leaving Seleucia Pierea, the seaport of Syrian Antioch, recounted in Acts 13:4, with Saul, Barnabus, and John Mark aboard, the high-risk voyage with Jesus to the ends of the earth sharing the good news of the kingdom is the vision of the church in the world. The ship on the voyage toward the kingdom is at home on a sea that is always out of human control, sometimes beautiful and peaceful, sometimes raging and violent, but always under the control of the Creator. This ship is at home on the sea.

THE LIFE OF FAITH IS LIKE SAILING

As the disciples discovered on the Sea of Galilee, and as Paul demonstrated so clearly in his post-conversion voyage of life and faith on the Mediterranean Sea, following Jesus both literally and figuratively involved sailing. Life is constantly unstable for those sailing on the sea and/or living by faith. It is a ceaseless balance between capsize and progress, exhilaration and alarm, ballast and sail. Constant adjustments in direction are necessary to at once utilize the power of the wind and avoid being capsized by it. Sailing and following Jesus are both risky endeavors. But for as long as the voyage lasts, this life is one of abundance of both rewards and suffering.

A successful voyage in the first century relied mostly on the captain, whose experience, memory, and wisdom, acquired through years of sailing, allowed him to recognize the visual reference points on land, discern the patterns of wind and wave, and make good judgments. But without the skill and courage of the crew in handling the ship, the voyage could just as easily end in disaster—which it often did, even with the best of captains and crews, because the sea cannot be predicted or controlled.

Charts and other navigational equipment came later. Paul's letters to the Christian communities in the seaports such as Ephesus, Corinth,

Philippi, and Thessaloniki, as well as John's Revelation, can be understood as navigational aids or early charts. But the presence of Jesus, the captain who had made the journey successfully; the gifts of discernment of the crew and all voyagers aboard; and the importance of the cooperation, quick obedience, and selflessness of everyone aboard the sailing vessel were understood by the seafaring Christians of the Mediterranean.

Aside from sophisticated instruments, instant communication, and superior equipment, nothing much has changed for sailors voyaging on literal or cultural seas. The most peaceful and comfortable sailing is downwind both at sea and in culture. But downwind is not necessarily the right direction. The destination may mean having to head up into the wind, in which case the gentle downwind instantly becomes a powerful, sometimes raging, fierce cross- or headwind. It is the same wind; the direction of the ship is what changes. As demonstrated by Jesus and experienced by Paul and John, so it is with following Jesus to the ends of the earth. And as Paul discovered more than once, shipwrecks occurred. But as Paul also discovered, shipwrecks were not the end of the journey, for Jesus is aboard and will bring his people home.

The seafaring followers of Jesus in the first century were like the seafarers of the Mediterranean have always been. They were flexible and resolute at the same time, for they knew that Jesus was Lord of land and sea and would win over all powers of evil on land and sea.

We must fearlessly go down to the sea again with Jesus. Jesus has brought us safe this far, and he will lead us home.

REFLECTIONS FROM THE LAND

Throughout this book, the image of an early sailing vessel has been used to indicate a personal story symbolizing the voyage of life and faith as we have experienced it so far. The early Christians of the Mediterranean seaports often used the image of a ship to symbolize the church.

They also used the anchor as a cross, representing Jesus, the anchor that is with his people on their voyage of faith and life. We found a small replica of an early Christian cross/anchor for sale in a catacomb in Rome (see fig. 12). For the early Christians, Jesus was the anchor that went to sea with them on their voyage of faith and life in the world. The alpha, the first letter of the Greek alphabet, represents the beginning of the voyage. The omega, the last letter of the Greek alphabet, represents the end. In between is the voyage on the perilous sea with the anchor, Jesus. Those early seafaring believers in Rome and other port cities of the Mediterranean recognized on their journey of life and faith in the raging conditions of "peace" in the Roman Empire that with the anchor they were safely at home everywhere. At any point of the voyage toward their true home port, they could always connect to safe harbors. There they could rest, recover, and share the good news. But they were never chained permanently to that place; they were bound for the kingdom.

Whether in the wilderness with the children of Israel, in a marginally seaworthy fishing boat on the Galilee in a storm, or even on the raging Mediterranean Sea, we are not alone. The presence of the Creator; of the Father, Son, and Holy Spirit on the face of the deep; of the One who is in control, dwells among his people on the move. We are at home on the journey anywhere in the world. The anchor is, like the tabernacle in the wilderness, like the "I am with you always" promise of Jesus, the working symbol of home on the voyage.

With brute power, cunning, and organization, Rome created *Mare Nostrum*. Every other sea empire since has continued the concept of trying to control the sea and in the process destroying it. Like the groaning earth, there is the possibility of no more degraded sea in the new creation, a vision of heaven and earth without a dead sea that we have polluted with oil and sewage, with islands of plastic garbage, an abused sea that humans have exploited, overfished, decimated, and used at times for bloody warfare with gigantic floating death machines of various navies and at other times used for entertaining the wealthy of the world aboard gigantic floating palaces. This sea will be no more, but rather, there will be a sea filled with the glory of God. From a sea of peril to a sea of promise, the *Mare Nostrum* of the Roman Empire will be, for the seafarers of faith, *Mare Domini* of the kingdom of God. There is no more sea to avoid.

But until then, the Spirit of God still hovers on the face of the deep as we voyage toward the vision of Scripture, moving us toward home, through the perils and promises of empires, toward the coming kingdom of God.

FIGURE 12: **Replica of an early Christian cross/anchor**

One day in Rome many years ago, Janet and I visited a catacomb. In the little gift shop at the end of the tour, we purchased the little replica and took it with us to *SailingActs*. Back aboard, we fastened it inside the cabin in a prominent location, where it remains to this day, reminding us, even when the sea is rough enough to throw us across the cabin unless we are hanging on, that Jesus is with us. No matter what happens, we can sail with confidence, even when afraid.

We found this early Christian understanding of Jesus so profoundly comforting—note the anchor and the letters are inside what appears to be a house rather than a ship, signifying the safety and security of home even at sea—that we decided to get a tattoo of this. This decision did not come easily. What about Leviticus 19:28? What about the negative view many Christians have of people with tattoos? But finally, being sailors who had taken some cues from Paul's understanding of the Law's application in the pagan world, and with an openness to participating in this traditional seafarer practice, we went to a tattoo parlor in the raucous port city of Marmaris, Turkey, when we were there to get them done. But upon arriving at the tattoo parlor and seeing the group of drunken US Navy sailors lined up for more tattoos to add to their impressive collections, we decided to think about our decision a bit longer.

Over the next couple of years, we thought about tattoos and how our Coptic Christian friends in Egypt had a Coptic cross tattooed on their right wrist. Those wishing to be publicly identified as a Christian will get the tattoo, an ancient tradition for Copts. For Christian adults in Egypt choosing to do so, getting the tattoo takes a certain kind of courage and commitment to identity in a country where Coptic Christians are a distinct minority, sometimes the object of discrimination and even violence by radical religious extremists.[3]

Several years after our near-tattoo experience in Turkey, we heard about a little tattoo shop in the Old City of Jerusalem, just inside Jaffa Gate. We discovered that the artist in that tattoo parlor was an Egyptian Coptic Christian who was part of a family who about three hundred years earlier had established this very business providing tattoos of the Jerusalem cross for pilgrims from Egypt. It seemed most appropriate to get our early Christian cross there, so we did.

At the end of fifteen months of sailing the routes of Paul, I concluded the journey to Rome, walking the last thirty miles (48 km) of the Appian Way, as Paul had, into the city. The following reflections are from Rome, written at the end of the journey in 2005.

> It was in the Mamertine Prison where I chose to end the voyage to Rome. I descended the steps inside the church of San Pietro in Carcere leading down into a simple cave cell. There were no tourists in Mamertine Prison, just a couple of Christian pilgrims from Bulgaria and an Italian couple holding hands. … Eventually they all left, and I sat alone in the cool, dark cell of the Roman prison with vivid images of sailing Acts. … I saw the glittering, attractive power and glory of Rome, and the fearsome power and astounding beauty of the sea. … I heard the shrieking of the wind in the rigging and the roar of

3. The process of tattooing among Egyptian Christians is an ancient tradition that dates back to the Coptic period of Egypt. The Coptic Orthodox Church in Egypt is one of the oldest Christian churches in the world. The Coptic cross tattoo publicly identifies the faith and particularly the courage of the Coptic believers in Egypt.

> the waves smashing against the cliffs of the Aegean islands. I heard the voices speaking Greek, Hebrew, Aramaic, Arabic, Turkish, Italian, and Maltese. Most were friendly, a few hostile. ... I tasted the oil and wine of the rim of the Mediterranean and the salt of the sea. I recalled the loneliness of voyaging; the fellowship of voyagers; the helpfulness of strangers; and the friendship of Jews and Greeks, pagans and Christians, Muslims, and atheists. I remembered the moments of desperation and fear, and days of living more intensely and joyfully than at any time in my life. Janet and I had followed Paul from Damascus to Rome. And like Paul, we had fought the good fight; we had finished our course.[4]

But we are not yet home. After twenty years of continuing to sail the Mediterranean Sea and the biblical story on *SailingActs* with my fearless first mate/wife Janet, we have learned to appreciate the wonderful, incredible biblical story from the perspective of the sea and its people. Our life and faith have been enriched by the fearless, skillful seafarers of the Mediterranean Sea, both Christian and pagan, ancient and modern. Seafarers of every tribe and tongue, like the descendants of Abraham, are created in God's image. Their sea-based cultures contribute to the fearless, outward-focused, universal understanding of the good news of Jesus, opening the door for all of us to be included in the kingdom of God.

We understand better what the promise of life in abundance means as we go with Jesus into the divided, unstable, uncontrollable, promising, and perilous world. We do not have to be afraid of the unknown. We cannot control the wind direction and storms of culture, only our responses. We cannot control the wind of the Spirit on the face of the deep, only our responses. We can trust and rely on God, and therefore ourselves, each other, and strangers. Life in

4. Linford Stutzman, *SailingActs: Following an Ancient Voyage* (Intercourse, PA: Good Books, 2006), 311.

abundance is full of blessings and suffering, but the blessings are far greater than the suffering.

We continue sailing the perilous seas toward the promised kingdom. We are at home in this world, for Jesus is with us. And we are not yet home.

BIBLIOGRAPHY

Abulafia, David. *The Great Sea: A Human History of the Mediterranean*. Oxford: Oxford University Press, 2011.

Arav, Rami, Richard A. Freund, and John F. Shroder Jr. "Bethsaida Rediscovered." *Biblical Archaeology Review* 26 (2000): 44–51, 53–56.

Ballard, Robert D., Lawrence E. Stager, Daniel Master, Dana Yoerger, David Mindell, Louis L. Whitcomb, Hanumant Singh, and Dennis Piechota. "Iron Age Shipwrecks in Deep Water off Ashkelon, Israel." *American Journal of Archaeology* 106.2 (2002): 151–68.

Beitzel, Barry J., ed. *Lexham Geographic Commentary on Acts through Revelation*. Bellingham, WA: Lexham Press, 2019.

Beitzel, Barry J. "Was There a Joint Nautical Venture on the Mediterranean Sea by Tyrian Phoenicians and Early Israelites?" *Bulletin of the American Schools of Oriental Research* 360 (2010): 37–66.

Beitzel, Barry J. *Where Was the Biblical Red Sea? Examining the Ancient Evidence*. Studies in Biblical Archaeology, Geography, and History. Bellingham, WA: Lexham Press, 2020.

Braudel, Fernand. *Memory and the Mediterranean*. New York: Knopf, 2001.

Braudel, Fernand. *The Mediterranean and the Mediterranean World in the Age of Philip II*. Translated by Siân Reynolds. New York: Harper & Row, 1972.

Cahill, Thomas. *Sailing the Wine-Dark Sea: Why the Greeks Matter*. New York: Anchor Books, 2004.

Casson, Lionel. *Ships and Seamanship in the Ancient World*. Baltimore, MD: The Johns Hopkins University Press, 1995.

Casson, Lionel. *The Ancient Mariners: Seafarers and Sea Fighters of the Mediterranean in Ancient Times*. 2nd ed. Princeton, NJ: Princeton University Press, 1991.

Casson, Lionel. *Travel in the Ancient World.* London: Allan & Unwin, 1974.

Cohen, Shaye J. D. "Did Ancient Jews Missionize?" *Biblical Review* 19 (2003): 40, 42–45, 47.

Cornell, Jimmy. *World Cruising Routes.* 4th ed. Camden, ME: International Marine, 1998.

Cosentino, Salvatore. "Mentality, Technology and Commerce: Shipping amongst the Mediterranean Islands in Late Antiquity and Beyond." Pages 65–76 in *The Insular System of the Early Byzantine Mediterranean.* Edited by Demetrios Michaelides, Philippe Pergola, and Enrico Zanini. British Archaeological Reports International Series 2523. Oxford: Archaeopress, 2013.

Dantas Gomes, Daniela Maria. "Mare Nostrum: Military History and Naval Power in Rome (2nd Century BCE–1st Century CE)." PhD dissertation, University of Lisbon, 2020. http://dx.doi.org/10.13140/RG.2.2.28353.38248.

deSilva, David A. "The Social and Geographical World of Ephesus." Pages 430–49 in Beitzel, *Lexham Geographic Commentary on Acts through Revelation.*

Diamond, Jared. *Guns, Germs, and Steel: The Fates of Human Societies.* New York: Norton, 2005.

Dothan, Trude, and Moshe Dothan. *People of the Sea: The Search for the Philistines.* New York: Macmillan, 1992.

Gadolou, Anastasia. "Life on Board." Pages 50–56 in *The Antikythera Shipwreck: The Ship, the Treasures, the Mechanism.* Edited by Nikolaos Kaltsas, Elena Vlachogianni, and Polyxeni Bouyia. Athens: Hellenic Ministry of Culture, National Archaeological Museum, 2012.

George, Rose. *90 Percent of Everything: Inside Shipping, the Invisible Industry That Puts Clothes on Your Back, Gas in Your Car, and Food on Your Plate.* New York: Metropolitan Books, 2013.

Habib, Shahnaz. *Airplane Mode: An Irreverent History of Travel.* New York: Catapult, 2023.

Hezser, Catherine. *Jewish Travel in Antiquity.* Tübingen: Mohr Siebeck, 2011.

Hezser, Catherine. "Travel and Mobility." Pages 210–26 in *Oxford Handbook for Jewish Daily Life in Roman Palestine.* Edited by Catherine Hezser. Oxford: Oxford University Press, 2010.

Hinrichsen, Don. *Our Common Seas: Coasts in Crisis*. London: Routledge, 1990.

Hirschfeld, Nicolle. "The Ship of Saint Paul: Historical Background." *Biblical Archaeologist* 53 (1990): 25–30.

Hoffmeier, James K. "Out of Egypt." *Biblical Archaeology Review* 33 (2007): 30–37, 39–41.

Hohlfelder, Robert L. "Caesarea Maritima: Herod the Great's City on the Sea." *National Geographic* 171 (1987): 260–79.

Hohlfelder, Robert L., and Robert L. Vann. "Cabotage at Aperlae in Ancient Lycia." *International Journal of Nautical Archaeology* 29 (2000): 126–35.

Josephus, Flavius. *The Works of Josephus: Complete and Unabridged*. Translated by William Whiston. Peabody, MA: Hendrickson, 1987.

Kashtan, Nadav. "Seafaring and Jews in Graeco-Roman Palestine: Realistic and Symbolic Dimensions." *Mediterranean Historical Review* 15 (2000): 16–28.

Knapp, Robert. *Invisible Romans*. Cambridge, MA: Harvard University Press, 2011.

Leidwanger, Justin. "Maritime Networks and Economic Regionalism in the Roman Eastern Mediterranean." *Les Nouvelles de l'archéologie* 135 (2014): 32–38.

Levinson, Marc. *The Box: How the Shipping Container Made the World Smaller and the World Economy Bigger*. Princeton, NJ: Princeton University Press, 2016. Kindle.

Ma, Guoqing. "Islands and the World from an Anthropological Perspective." *International Journal of Anthropology and Ethnology* 4 (2020). https://doi.org/10.1186/s41257-020-00038-x.

Malina, Bruce. *The New Testament World: Insights from Cultural Anthropology*. 3rd ed. Louisville: Westminster John Knox, 2001.

McGrail, Seán. *Boats of the World: From the Stone Age to Medieval Times*. Oxford: Oxford University Press, 2001.

Mendels, Doron. "Why Paul Went West." *Biblical Archaeology Review* 37 (2011): 49–54, 68.

Murphy-O'Connor, Jerome. *St. Paul's Ephesus: Texts and Archaeology*. Collegeville, MN: Liturgical Press, 2008.

Notley, Steven R., and Mordechai Aviam. "Searching for Bethsaida: The Case for El-Araj." *Biblical Archaeology Review* 46 (2020): 28–39.

Oleson, John Peter. "The Evolution of Harbour Engineering in the Ancient Mediterranean World." Pages 509–22 in *Harbors and Harbor Cities in the Eastern Mediterranean from Antiquity to the Byzantine Period: Recent Discoveries and Current Approaches*. Edited by Sabine Ladstaetter, Felix Pirson, and Thomas Schmidts. Istanbul: Ege Yayinlari, 2014.

Otto, Rudolf. *The Idea of the Holy*. Translated by John W. Harvey. Oxford: Oxford University Press, 1923.

Patai, Raphael. *The Children of Noah: Jewish Seafaring in Ancient Times*. Princeton, NJ: Princeton University Press, 1998.

Perrottet, Tony. *Pagan Holiday: On the Trail of Ancient Roman Tourists*. New York: Random House, 2003.

Powley, Helen R., Phillip von Cappellen, and Michael D. Krom. "Nutrient Cycling in the Mediterranean Sea: The Key to Understanding How the Unique Marine Ecosystem Functions and Responds to Anthropogenic Pressures." In *Mediterranean Identities: Environment, Society, Culture*. Edited by Borna Fuerst-Bjeliš. London: IntechOpen, 2017. https://doi.org/10.5772/intechopen.70878.

Quezada, Zeke. "Mediterranean Mooring: What Is It and Why?" American Association of Sailing. https://asa.com/news/2023/01/10/mediterranean-mooring-what-is-it-and-why/.

Rackham, Oliver, "The Physical Setting." Pages 33–65 in *The Mediterranean in History*. Edited by David Abulafia. London: Thames and Hudson, 2003.

Rauh, Nicholas K. *Merchants, Sailors and Pirates in the Roman World*. Stroud, UK: Tempus, 2003.

Rauh, Nicholas K., Matthew J. Dillon, and T. Davina McClain. "*Ochlos Nautikos:* Leisure Culture and Underclass Discontent in the Roman Maritime World." Pages 197–242 in *The Maritime World of Ancient Rome: Proceedings of "The Maritime World of Ancient Rome" Conference Held at the American Academy in Rome 27–29 March 2003*. Edited by Robert L. Hohlfelder. Ann Arbor, MI: University of Michigan Press, 2008.

Rediker, Marcus. *Between the Devil and the Deep Blue Sea*. Cambridge: Cambridge University Press, 1987.

Schnabel, Eckard J. "Jesus' Missionary Commission and the Ends of the Earth." Pages 51–67 in Beitzel, *Lexham Geographic Commentary on Acts through Revelation.*

Schörle, Katia. "Constructing Port Hierarchies: Harbours of the Central Tyrrhenian Coast." Pages 93–106 in *Maritime Archaeology and Ancient Trade in the Mediterranean.* Edited by Damian Robinson and Andrew Wilson. Oxford: Oxford Centre for Maritime Archaeology, 2011.

Shalvi, Golan, and Ayelet Gilboa. "Between Israel and Phoenicia: The Iron IIA–B Fortified Purple-Dye Production Centre at Tel Shiqmona." *Tel Aviv* 50 (2023): 75–110. https://doi.org/10.1080/03344355.2023.2190283.

Stager, Lawrence E. "When Canaanites and Philistines Ruled Ashkelon." *Biblical Archaeology Review* 17 (1991): 24–29, 31, 35–37, 40–42.

Stark, Rodney. *Cities of God: The Real Story of How Christianity Became an Urban Movement and Conquered Rome.* San Francisco: HarperSanFrancisco, 2006.

Sternman, Baruch. *The Rarest Blue: The Remarkable Story of an Ancient Color Lost to History and Rediscovered.* 2nd ed. Jerusalem: Ptil Tekhelet, 2017.

Stutzman, Linford. *SailingActs: Following an Ancient Voyage.* Intercourse, PA: Good Books, 2006.

Thurston, Herbert. "Symbolism." Pages 373–77 in vol. 14 of *The Catholic Encyclopedia.* New York: Robert Appleton Company, 1912.

Trinka, Erik. "To Sea or Not to Sea? That is the Question. Jewish Perceptions of Seafaring in Ancient Palestine." Unpublished manuscript, 2012.

Tülek, Füsun. "Northeastern Harbors of the Mediterranean Sea on the Cilician Coast and Gulf of Issikos." Pages 413–24 in *Connecting Cultures: Trade and Interconnections in Ancient Near East from the Beginning until the End of the Roman Period.* Edited by Vasıf Şahoğlu, Müge Şevketoğlu, and Yiğit H. Erbil. Ankara: Ankara University Press, 2019.

Wachsman, Shelly. *The Sea of Galilee Boat.* College Station, TX: Texas A&M University Press, 2009.

Wade, Janet. "Sailors, Merchants and the Maritime Cults that Sailed into the Ports (and Streets) of Early Byzantium." Pages 269–87 in

Byzantium, Its Neighbours and Its Cultures. Byzantina Australiensia 20. Edited by Danijel Dzino and Ken Parry. Leiden: Brill, 2014.

Wilson, Andrew. "Developments in Mediterranean Shipping and Maritime Trade from the Hellenistic Period to AD 1000." Pages 33–60 in *Maritime Archaeology and Ancient Trade in the Mediterranean*. Edited by Damian Robinson and Andrew Wilson. Oxford: Oxford Centre for Maritime Archaeology, 2011.

Wilson, Andrew, and Damian Robinson. "Introduction: Maritime Archaeology and the Ancient Economy." Pages 1–11 in *Maritime Archaeology and Ancient Trade in the Mediterranean*. Edited by Damian Robinson and Andrew Wilson. Oxford: Oxford Centre for Maritime Archaeology, 2011.

Wilson, Mark. "Geography of the Island of Patmos." Pages 619–28 in Beitzel, *Lexham Geographic Commentary on Acts through Revelation*.

Wilson, Mark. *Victory through the Lamb: A Guide to Revelation in Plain Language*. Wooster, OH: Weaver, 2014.

Wright, Paul. "The Geography of Caesarea Maritima." Pages 202–21 in Beitzel, *Lexham Geographic Commentary on Acts through Revelation*.

Wright, Paul. *Understanding the New Testament: An Introductory Atlas*. Jerusalem: Carta, 2004.

APPENDIX

NAUTICAL TERMS IN LUKE

ACTS	KJV	GREEK	TRANS-LITERATION	INFERRED DEFINITIONS IN CONTEXT	USE IN ACTS	USE IN LUKE
10:11	sheet	ὀθόνη	othonē	linen cloth (sail)	X	
13:4	sailed	ἀποπλέω	apopleō	sail away, depart by ship, set sail	X	
15:39	sailed	ἐκπλέω	ekpleō	to sail from, sail away	X	
16:11	straight course	εὐθυδρομέω	euthydromeō	to make a straight course	X	
20:16	sail by	παραπλέω	parapleō	(1) sail by, sail past	X	
21:3	unlade	ἀποφορτίζομαι	apophortizomai	(1) unload, or lighten a ship	X	
21:3	sailed	πλέω	pleō	(1) to sail, navigate, travel by ship	X	X
21:7	course	πλόος	ploos	(1) voyage	X	
27:10	lading	φόρτος	phortos	(1) load of a ship	X	
27:11	owner of the ship	ναύκληρος	nauklēros	(1) ship owner, ship master	X	
27:12	northwest	χῶρος	chōros	(1) northwest wind	X	
27:12	southwest	λίψ	lips	(1) southwest wind	X	
27:13	blew softly	ὑποπνέω	hypopneō	(2) to blow softly	X	
27:14	Euroclydon	εὐρακύλων	eurakylōn	(1) south east wind raising mighty waves	X	
27:14	tempestuous	τυφωνικός	typhōnikos	(1) like a hurricane, tempestuous	X	
27:15	bear up	ἀντοφθαλμέω	antophthalmeō	(2) bear up	X	
27:16	running under	ὑποτρέχω	hypotrechō	(1) to run past, run in lee of	X	
27:16	boat	σκάφη	skaphē	(2) boat	X	
27:17	undergirding	ὑποζώννυμι	hypozōnnymi	(2) to bind a ship with cables to help survive storm	X	
27:17	quicksand	Σύρτις	Syrtis	(1) Syrtis—by inference, sandbar	X	
27:18	tossed with a tempest	χειμάζω	cheimazō	(1) to toss about upon the waves	X	
27:18	lightened	ἐκβολή	ekbolē	(1) throw goods overboard to lighten the ship	X	
27:19	tackling	σκευή	skeuē	(1) the equipment or tackling of a ship	X	
27:28	sounded	βολίζω	bolizō	(1) to heave a lead weight to take a depth-sounding	X	

ACTS	KJV	GREEK	TRANS-LITERATION	INFERRED DEFINITIONS IN CONTEXT	USE IN ACTS	USE IN LUKE
27:28	(20) fathoms	ὀργυιά	orgyia	(1) distance of reach, about 5–6 feet	X	
27:28	rocks	τραχύς	trachys	(1) rocky places in the sea (reef?)	X	X
27:30	foreship	πρῷρα	prōra	(1) bow of a ship	X	
27:38	lightened	κουφίζω	kouphizō	(1) to lighten the ship by throwing cargo overboard	X	
27:39	thrust in	ἐξωθέω	exōtheō	(1) to thrust, propel	X	
27:4	sailed over	διαπλέω	diapleō	(1) to sail across	X	
27:4	sailed under	ὑποπλέω	hypopleō	(1) to sail close by, under (2) to sail leeward	X	
27:40	mainsail	ἀρτέμων	artemōn	(1) top sail or main sail	X	
27:40	bands	ζευκτηρία	zeuktēria	(1) band, fastener	X	
27:41	where two seas met	διθάλασσος	dithalassos	(1) place where two seas meet, isthmus, reef	X	
27:41	ran aground	ἐπικέλλω	epikellō	(1) to run a ship aground	X	
27:41	stuck fast	ἐρείδω	ereidō	(1) fix firmly, stick fast	X	
27:41	ship	ναῦς	naus	(1) a large ship	X	
27:42	swim	ἐκκολυμβάω	ekkolymbaō	(1) to swim out of	X	
27:43	cast themselves	ἀπορρίπτω	aporriptō	(2) to cast oneself	X	
27:43	swim	κολυμβάω	kolymbaō	(1) dive, swim	X	
27:44	boards	σανίς	sanis	(1) a board, plank	X	
27:5	sea	πέλαγος	pelagos	(1) the sea (2) high sea, deep sea	X	
27:7	sailed slowly	βραδυπλοέω	bradyploeō	(1) to sail slowly	X	
27:7	(not) suffering	προσεάω	proseaō	(1) to permit to approach or arrive	X	
27:8	(fair) havens	λιμήν	limēn	(1) harbor, haven	X	
27:8	hardly passing	παραλέγομαι	paralegomai	(1) to sail past, coast along (2) work past	X	
28:11	Castor and Pollux	Διόσκουροι	Dioskouroi	(1) Castor and Pollux, special protectors of sailors	X	
28:11	sign	παράσημος	parasēmos	(4) a ship marked with a sign	X	
				TOTALS	**48**	**2**

FREQUENCY OF REFERENCES TO "SEA(S)" IN HEBREW SCRIPTURE

	HEBREW SCRIPTURES	APOCRYPHA	GREEK SCRIPTURES	TOTAL
Red Sea or Red Sea Event	63	7	4	74
Unspecified Sea or Seas	100	23	29	152
Sea as Metaphor	12	18	10	40
Mediterranean Sea by Any Name	99	20	13	132
Dead Sea	16	4	0	20
Sea of Galilee	10	1	40	51

Notes: The largest number of references to seas are unnamed seas, or used to mention sea generically.

The Mediterranean is never mentioned by its current name but by the other names used, and the context makes it clear when the Mediterranean is being referenced.

In the Hebrew Scriptures, the Sea of Galilee is referred to as a geographical/political/tribal boundary orientation only. In the Greek New Testament, it is only mentioned in reference to Jesus and his followers.

PAUL'S LIFETIME ON LAND AND SEA

	HOME BASE CITIES			TRAVELING AND TEMPORARY OR INVOLUNTARY STAYS						DISTANCES TRAVELED	
	Time in Port	Time Inland		Time in Seaport Cities		Time at Sea	Time on Road	Time in Inland Cities		Sea Distances	Land Distances
	Years	Days	Years	Days	Months	Days	Days	Days	Months	Miles	Miles
Birth to First Mission	27	75	20	29		39	70			1,696	1,183
Journey 1	1	30		90		28	77		6	1,120	1,255
Journey 2	1			100	18	32	77		11	1,813	1,284
Journey 3				142	30	27	37	81		1,353	1,769
Caesarea, Voyage to Rome, and Rome				93	48	49	15	30		1,850	170
Totals	29 Years	0.29 Years	20 Years	1.24 Years	8 Years	0.4 Years	0.76 Years	0.3 Years	1.42 Years	7,832 Miles	5,661 Miles

LIFETIME AT HOME BASES

Years in Port Cities	29
Years in Inland Cities	20.29
Total Years at Home Bases	49.29

LIFETIME TRAVELING ON LAND/SEA

Years Aboard Ships / at Ports	9.24
Years on Roads / in Cities	2.48
Total Years Traveling	11.72

LIFETIME MILES TRAVELED

Miles at Sea	7,832
Miles Over Land	5,661
Total Travels	13,493

ESTIMATED LIFETIME TOTALS

Years in Ships / Ports	38.24
Years Inland	22

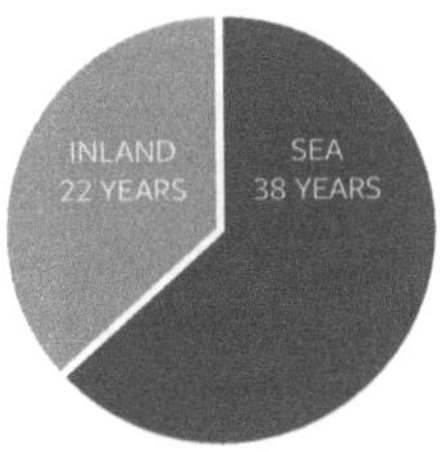

NAME AND SUBJECT INDEX

SCRIPTURE INDEX